"From Blyth to B - and back."

CW00408963

Part One

Henry G Dobson

"…if the mind be not in the habit of serious employment it will lose its energy and those powers a man may have been blessed with will entirely vanish."

(George III, in a letter to his son, Prince Augustus, in 1770, when the young seventeen year old Prince was residing in the south of France.)

"George III", by Stanley Ayling: published by Collins in 1972.

Preface

From the moment the idea of writing a book like this began to germinate in my mind (or, more accurately, my 'mind's eye') I realised there would be minor difficulties.

If, as was my intention, I resolved to travel the Coastal Route, from Blyth to Berwick then return south down the A1 Trunk Road I must bear in mind the fact that there are more than fifty hamlets, villages and towns lying within approximately a mile or so of their respective highways – which of these was I prepared to include in my odyssey and which others, sadly, was I disposed to leave out?

Since the book was never intended to be a comprehensive travelogue it was clearly impossible to include all the locations alluded to without ending up with a 'volume' the size of an encyclopaedia.

Yet anyone who is familiar with this part of our beloved Northumberland, especially the attractions of its beautiful coastline, will verify that I was literally spoiled for choice – for on closer examination I was able to confirm what I had long suspected …. every one of these delightful localities, whether town or small village, had so much to interest and attract the intrepid photographer, amateur or professional.

My dilemma (for this is most certainly what it was) lay in deciding firstly, which location had most to offer and, secondly, which of its 'special attractions' appealed to me, personally.

This choice, of both location and subject was, in the circumstances, both individual and arbitrary – though it was strongly influenced by my early decision to photograph, as far as possible, subjects which were both a trifle unusual and which had been featured comparatively infrequently in other publications.

In some instances this presented me with something of a dichotomy. For example, how could I include the charming medieval village of

Warkworth without photographic reference to its castle, about which so many excellent books have already been exhaustively written and illustrated?

The castle dominates the village; it has a fascinating history; it is instantly recognised by the thousands of visitors who flock to Warkworth each year and, architecturally, it is one of the most important buildings in the North of England.

The same, of course, can be said of the castles at Dunstanburgh, in the ancient market town of Alnwick and on the romantic, wind-swept island of Lindisfarne.

The fact is that to ignore such conspicuous and distinguished landmarks would be perverse and to deliberately disregard them, in a book of this nature, would be pure folly.

I have not, therefore, overlooked these celebrated 'monuments' but have, nevertheless, focused my attention on less familiar subjects in what may be described as 'less well publicised locations' – the wind turbines at North Blyth; the surface buildings at Woodhorn Colliery Museum; Morpeth's fine Castle Gatehouse; dovecotes at Embleton; a lighthouse in a back street in Blyth; medieval grave covers in a church in Newbiggin and the Governor's house in Berwick (a town, incidentally, where one building in ten is 'Grade listed') – and so on.

If there were difficulties in deciding what to include in the book, from an almost unbelievable choice of subjects, any disappointment lay only in the knowledge that I had to rigorously curtail my natural inclination to take far more photographs than I could reasonably expect to have published. Discipline and restraint were meant to be my watchwords. I must confess I often succumbed to temptation.

That said, my rewards have been manifold.

It has been my wonderful good fortune to be given the opportunity to photograph some of the loveliest houses in Northumberland – at Doxford, Craster, Swarland, Acton, Bockenfield, Embleton, Preston, Adderstone and many more. I have been privileged to meet their owners who welcomed me with kindness and interest. I am indebted to all these good souls who so graciously allowed me to include pictures of their lovely homes and to others whose responsibility it is to safeguard the well-being of 'public' properties.

Inevitably, readers will criticise my choice of subjects – this is their prerogative. They may well find fault with the quality and composition of my photographs: this, too, is their rightful privilege. As an amateur, possessing none of the expensive accoutrements so essential for professional colleagues I am painfully aware of both my shortcomings and my limitations: I beg my critics, therefore, to exercise a little charity.

In the final analysis judgements are about opinions and preferences: perish the thought that our tastes and fancies should be the same. But if, while flicking through the pages of the book, readers occasionally pause to remark, "I've never seen that before:" or, "I didn't know that was there:" if a picture arouses curiosity or sparks good natured debate, or it focuses your attention, even for only a few moments, then it will surely have served its purpose and justified its being there.

I hope, more than anything, it will excite your interest.

Acknowledgements

I am greatly indebted to the following individuals and organisations for their kind permission to publish my photographs

Part 1:

British Holidays, The Castle (Haggerston): English Heritage, Ravensdowne Barracks (Berwick): The National Trust, the Castle and The Lime Kilns (Holy Island): The Brethren of Trinity House, The Navigational Beacons (Guile Point, Ross Sands): Mr F W A Watson-Armstrong, The Castle (Bamburgh): The Royal National Lifeboat Institution, The Grace Darling Museum (Bamburgh): The National Trust, The Farne Islands and the Lime Kilns (Beadnell): Mr K J Seymour-Walker, Embleton Towers (Embleton): English Heritage, The Castle (Dunstanburgh): L Robson & Sons Ltd, The Smoke House (Craster): Mrs Fiona and Miss Mary Craster, The Tower Mansion House (Craster): English Heritage, The Castle (Warkworth): The Royal Society for the Protection of Birds, Coquet Island: Reverend Judith M Grieve, the interior of St Bartholomew's Church (Newbiggin-by-the-Sea): Wansbeck District Council, The Colliery Museum and St Mary's Church (Woodhorn): The Royal National Lifeboat Institution, The Lifeboat House (Newbiggin-by-the-Sea): Mr Simon Pringle, Centre Manager, The Keel Row Shopping Centre, The Statue of 'Willie' Carr (Blyth).

Part 2:

Welbeck Estates Co Ltd, The Castle (Bothal): The Landmark Trust, The Castle Gatehouse (Morpeth): Mr and Mrs I Elliott, Horsley Tower (Longhorsley): Mr Bernard Bloodworth, Linden Hall (Longhorsley): Mr Trevor Thorne, Embleton Hall (Longframlington): Mr and Mrs T N H Sanderson, Eshott Hall (Eshott): Dr Maureen Hughes, The Manor House (Bockenfield): Mr and Mrs Brian Reed, Thirston House (West Thirston, Felton): Mr and Mrs D Moore, Acton House (Acton, Old Felton): Mr and Mrs Mark Goodyear, Acton Hall (Acton, Old Felton): Mr and Mrs A Proctor, The Old Hall (Swarland): Cpt F N H Widdrington, The Hall (Newton-on-the-Moor): Mr C J Bosanquet, The Hall (Rock, Alnwick): Mr and Mrs Brian Burnie, The Hall (Doxford): Major T H Baker-Cresswell, The Tower and Mansion House (Preston): Mr David Radliff, The Hall (Adderstone): Belford Hall Management Company, The Hall (Belford): Mrs Margaret and Mr John Riddell, West Hall (Belford): Mr Paul Shirley, The Blue Bell Inn (Belford).

Special thanks to my wife, Susan, for her wonderful support; to Pat Hughes for kindly scanning my type and to Ron Hodgson for his many hours of invaluable technical assistance – thank you all.

The old staithes with the Power Station (now decommissioned) in the background.

View from Battleship Wharf.

Two of the wind turbines situated just off the east pier.

Blyth Harbour Wind Farm (owned by the Blyth Harbour Commission) was conceived and engineered by Border Wind, who now operate the wind farm. Commissioned in January 1993 the nine 300kw wind turbines supply a maximum of 2.7 MW in the local grid network.

Just over half a mile offshore are the two first fully offshore wind turbines anywhere in the United Kingdom.

Alumia Silos

Alumina from Canada is unloaded at the port and stored in these huge, orange silos from where it is taken, by rail and in powder form, to be processed at the Lynemouth Smelter.

Wind turbines on the east pier.

William ('Willie') Carr   (Blyth)

This veritable 'Samson' was born on April 23rd, 1756.

As a young lad he began his working life as a blacksmith's apprentice, an occupation for which he was admirably suited for by the time he was seventeen he was already six feet three inches (1.87m) tall, with broad, muscular shoulders and weighed no less than sixteen stones (more than 100k). He was rightly proud of his fine physique though, like so many men of his outstanding build he was a gentle, kind man.

On February 15th, 1783, he married Jane Brown, a native of Blyth. One year later the first of their two daughters, Francis, was born; the second, Amy was born four years after her sister.

The nature of William's work did much to develop and strengthen his stature. By the time he was thirty he had grown another inch taller and now weighted twenty-four stones (150k). All of it was solid bone and muscle and yet, for a man of his incredible bulk, Carr was remarkably agile.

To demonstrate his fitness he once vaulted a five-barred gate, using only one hand, while carrying an eight stone (50k) woman tucked under his arm. But Willie was not just a man of unusual strength; he had a good brain to accompany his prodigious, physical capabilities.

Having some years earlier completed his apprenticeship and learned his trade well he eventually left the employer he had served faithfully and established his own business in Blyth.

First and foremost he fashioned harpoons for the whaling ships sailing from ports on the North-East coast. Indeed, such was Willie's reputation for the fine manufacture of these implements that whaling crews insisted on having their gear made by William Carr of Blyth and believed themselves seriously disadvantaged if they set sail without it.

William ('Willie') Carr   (Blyth)

Photographed by kind permission of Mr Simon Pringle (Centre Manager).

The statue stands in the middle of the Keel Row shopping centre.

A number of stories are told illustrating Willie's phenomenal strength and it is these which have established him, for all time, as one of Blyth's legendary characters.

Carr was by no means an aggressive man by nature and though his vanity occasionally prompted him to demonstrate his skills he was, in every sense, a "gentle giant".

There is not one single recording of him flaunting his great strength meanly, for selfish reasons, or of him taking deliberate advantage of any man obviously his physical inferior.

More than once he was called upon to restore derailed coal-wagons back on the lines where they belonged. Using his strong back he would lift one end of the wagon at a time (entirely unaided) until the wayward vehicle was back where it should have been.

On one occasion he was confronted by a gang of ne'er-do-wells, with a donkey, whilst he was peacefully strolling the banks of the River Blyth. They were clearly intent on mischief and doubtless felt encouraged by the fact that there were six of them. Willie, rather than become involved in an unseemly brawl, simply picked up their donkey and deposited the startled creature in a nearby coal-wagon. The blacksmith then sauntered off nonchalantly continuing his stroll and leaving his would-be assailants to wonder at his formidable strength and consider how best to rescue their helpless donkey. He was hired to repair the broken anchor chain of a ship (the Minerva) docked in Blyth harbour. He waited and waited for the chain to arrive at his forge until finally, running out of patience, he set off to discover the cause of the delay. Approaching the dockside he spotted five sailors struggling, unsuccessfully, to move the ship's anchor. Willie, unceremoniously, picked up the anchor, laid it across his back and with the chain trailing along behind him he returned to his forge to complete his allotted task: the anchor weighed half a tonne!

On numerous occasions, as a celebrated local figure, he was invited to Seaton Delaval Hall to entertain his lordship's guests by performing various feats of strength. Once, the 'entertainment' was to take the form of a boxing match between Willie and a prize-fighter by the name of 'Big Ben'. A ring was erected, a referee and seconds were appointed and the two huge men confronted each other in the centre of the ring. Both were instructed to "shake hands and come out fighting".

However, Carr's handshake was so powerful that he burst the fingertips of his opponent and there was blood everywhere. Despite the taunts of Lord Delaval's guests Ben could not be persuaded to take part in the fight declaring "he would rather be kicked by a horse than receive a blow from Willie's huge fist".

William Carr never regarded sleep as an essential factor when work was concerned.

The Monthly Chronicles of 1887 record that he once worked 132 consecutive hours, stopping only for food, drink and the needs of Nature. Then, after sleeping solidly for 12 hours, he resumed his task and continued working for a further 120 hours.

This remarkable character passed away on the 6th of September, 1825, in his sixtieth year.

The Roman Catholic Church of Our Lady and St Wilfred   (Blyth)

The first Roman Catholic Church to be built in Blyth (1863).

"A handsome stone building in the Early English style (14th century), having a polygonal apse chancel containing three beautiful, stained glass windows by Bennett of Newcastle. It was to be served by priests of the English Benedictine Congregation. A new high altar was erected in 1878, at a cost of £400, to commemorate the opening of the church fifteen years previously."

A covered walk, or cloister, links the transept with buildings to the east 'which formally housed a small community of Benedictine monks'.

16 Arthur Street   (Blyth)

An attractive building, standing on the corner of Arthur Street and Waterloo Road.

Once a Convent and later a home for retired nuns it presently houses a group of young people, drawn not only from around Europe but from much further afield (the Philippines, South Africa, etc) who have volunteered to give at least one year of their lives in order the spread the message of Jesus Christ in Catholic schools and other organisations within the diocese. They have a roof over their heads and they receive all their meals but they have all given up their jobs to do this admirable work.

The Boathouse Tavern   (Blyth)

Probably the oldest building in Blyth

Originally the Brewery Bar. The Blyth Brewery was built in 1784-86 at a cost of £1,340-13-9 and was owned by Sir Matthew White Ridley. Sir Matthew operated the brewery for nine and a half years before he decided to lease it to a succession of other operators.

This brewery was built to replace a smaller brewery in Queen's Lane also owned and operated by Ridley.

Due to wartime restrictions the brewery was forced to close in 1916 and it never re-opened. The plant was sold off in the late 1930s and part of the building was demolished.

The Brewery Bar became the Pilot Cutter in 1967 and in April 1979, it again changed its name to the Boathouse Tavern.

This late 17th century building, with its open pedimented gable above openings in architraves with triangular or segmental pediments, was part of a big brewery complex in the 19th century.

The Harbour Commissioners' Building   (Blyth)

Built in 1903 the Office stands on the corner of Bridge Street and Plessey Road. The ground floor is of ashlar with channelled rustication: the two floors above are of brick though the window dressings are all of stone. The arcaded entrance is flanked by oval windows draped with garlands with a pair of Roman Doric pillars either side of the door. The offices were opened by Sir Matthew White Ridley on the 17th July 1913.

The King's Head

The first building on this site was open before 1821 (it is mentioned in the 1822 Trade Directory and Recognizance Book). That particular building was demolished in August 1892: it was rebuilt and opened in 1893.

The Steamboat Inn   **(Blyth)**

The Star and Garter Inn, Northumberland Street (now Bridge Street) is said to date from the early 18th century. The early Methodists in Blyth held their meetings in the long rooms of the Star and Garter. This old inn was demolished in August 1892 and a larger inn built on the site. The name changed to the Steamboat Inn on May the 5th, 1967.

The Oddfellow's Arms

The old Oddfellow's Arms is listed in the Trade Directory of 1841.The present inn, on Bridge Street, was rebuilt in 1887.

The High Light   (Blyth)

The 'Lighthouse in the street' stands in the back lane of Bath Terrace, Blyth. It was built in 1788 by Sir Matthew White Ridley, the owner of Cowpen Colliery, who has his own staith for shipping coal: at that time it stood only ten metres from the shoreline of the river.

When the lighthouse was first built it had a coal-fire on the top for a light: this was replaced by an oil-lamp near the beginning of the 19th century and the lighthouse was heightened, hence the lower of the square windows.

In 1857 the light was changed from oil to gas and the building was again heightened in the 1880s when the South Harbour was being constructed. This light was not converted to electricity until the 1960s. It no longer functions as a lighthouse.

The remaining standing structures: after the colliery closed in 1981 more than half the surface buildings were pulled down.

The Colliery Museum   **(Woodhorn)**

Shaft sinking began in Woodhorn in 1894 and the first coal was drawn to the surface four years later. In 1916, an underground explosion killed thirteen men: a memorial to their memory stands in the museum's car park. In 1924, 2,577 people worked in Woodhorn Colliery. The pit closed in 1981 and more than half the surface buildings were demolished before it was decided to turn the site into a museum and country park. The museum opened in 1989. All the buildings are of yellow, Ashington bricks made from clay brought out of the colliery. Woodhorn is now regarded as one of the most important preserved collieries in England.

The Banner Hall where the miners' banners are displayed. Here, too, can be seen memorabilia of the disaster of 1916.

The (1923) Memorial to the thirteen victims killed in the Woodhorn Colliery disaster of August 13th, 1916.

The number one shaft tower and winding wheel with the number one
Winding House behind it.

Number one shaft tower and winding wheel and the Jack Engine House
of c. 1895

The Jack Engine House of c.1895 with the shaft towers and winding wheels to the left and right.

Number 2 Heapstead and Fanhouse (1895/1900) – foreground, left of centre: behind it the Winding House number 2 (of c.1900)

The Colliery Museum   (Woodhorn)

The narrow gauge railway.

The workshop block, built around 1895. Here can be seen mining and social history displays, a football exhibition, art galleries, a children's activity area and so on. The building running from left to right is the stable block.

Photographed by kind permission of Wansbeck District Council.

Church of St Mary   (Woodhorn)

Founded more than 1200 years ago, in Saxon times, St Mary's is said to be the oldest church on the Northumbrian coast. It was altered and enlarged many times during the first five centuries of its existence.

Now, alas, only a few traces of Saxon, Norman and Gothic architecture can still be seen. The piers and arch of the Tower, the turret stairs and part of the nave, on the north side, are Saxon. The two round arches separating the nave from the north aisle are Norman. Two other round arches, resting on taller columns, on the other side of the church and three walls of the Tower, are all late 12th century.

During the church's restoration (1842-43) all the exterior masonry, save that of the two lower stages of the west tower, and all the windows were replaced with new.

Photographed by kind permission of Wansbeck District Council.

The base of the Tower may possibly be 11th century. The upper parts were a part of the mid-19th century restoration and have been bitingly described as "rather atrocious neo-Norman with an absurdly top-heavy arcaded parapet". The arms of the Widdringtons and the Ogles can be seen on the outside of the Tower's west wall.

Newbiggin-by-the-Sea

Newbiggin, way back in history, was originally called South Wellerick. The name changed over the centuries from Neubegang to Newbegining, and so on, until finally it became Newbiggin. In the fourteenth century it was a maritime town of some importance. In the wars between Edward II of England and his northern neighbour, Scotland, 'Newbyggyng' was obliged to provide a ship 'for naval purposes'. Edward stayed here on at least two occasions. In 1352 we know it had a harbour, with a pier on the north side. The harbour must have been of fairly deep water since vessels of considerable tonnage were able to shelter and trade, to and from here – corn was shipped from Newbiggin in fairly large quantities. But is seems quite possible there was some prehistoric settlement here for, in 1875, while making a cutting to the seashore three bronze spearheads were discovered. As a small boy who lived through the austere years of the 1940s it was always a special treat to visit Newbiggin. As the bus approached the small seaside town the excitement grew. The sight of the sun shimmering on the blue sea and the pungent aroma of seaweed and kelp heralded our imminent arrival and a day of joy and happiness such as today's young people can barely imagine – and all for the price of a sixpenny bus fare, a packet of egg sandwiches and a bottle of Muter's lemonade. In those days, when distressing memories of a recent war and the inescapable restrictions of rationing brought despair and sometimes hardship, the children were unsurprisingly oblivious of all these problems and lived, as children always have, in their own little world of sheltered innocence. Scores of families would make their way to Newbiggin to spend a day on the lovely golden sands. There were boat trips around the bay, twelve or more passengers aboard a stout Northumbrian coble, its Union Jack flag fluttering proudly and defiantly in a stiff, offshore breeze. There were donkey rides and "shuggy-boats" and a gay little roundabout (or carousel, as it is now grandly called). Deck chairs and green canvas tents could be hired for the day and there was a shelter or 'pavilion' on the promenade, with toilets, where you could obtain hot water. The sea front was very different then.

'Denis', a retired fisherman (aged 74) who has sadly watched his beloved fishing industry decline over the years until now fewer than ten boats represent Newbiggin's fishing 'fleet'.

All these things have gone now; the deck-chairs, the donkeys – and, sadly, most of the beach. Day trippers no longer flock to Newbiggin to 'plodge' in the sea and relax in the sunshine, their knotted hankies warding off sunstroke while the 'bairns' built their sandcastles or begged, repeatedly, for an ice-cream from Bertorelli's. Though you can still buy crabs or prawns in small fresh fish shops in the town the once thriving fishing industry has all but disappeared – over-fishing and quotas imposed by the bureaucrats in Brussels have seen to that.

Once upon a time Newbiggin boasted a fleet of almost a hundred fishing boats. Over the years this number has dwindled: fifty, thirty, twenty… and now there are fewer than ten. Six boats put out to sea in Winter (weather permitting) to catch crabs, lobsters and prawns. In June eight vessels leave the bay to catch salmon: the 'salmon season' lasts three months. The outlook for the few remaining families whose livelihood depends on this once thriving trade is uncertain, to say the least, and as it is in so many of our small ports and coastal villages. Various factors combined to hasten Newbiggin's demise as a small but successful seaside resort. Paradoxically, the sea, which washed away so much of the beach and threw up in its stead shingle and large stones: the coal industry made its own ruinous contribution and the increased prosperity of ordinary working people who, for as long as anyone could remember, had happily spent their days-away holidays on the beaches of Newbiggin, Blyth or Whitley Bay. A fortune has been spent on strengthening and improving the town's sea-defences and an excellent job has been done upgrading the promenade. Both these projects will, I'm sure, bring comfort to the good people of the town and a degree of justifiable satisfaction and pride to the local authorities. But whereas the forces of Nature will have their way (often despite Man's best endeavours) those who knowingly contributed to the destruction of what was a fine, clean, sandy beach ought to have been ashamed of themselves. As people grew increasingly more affluent and the privations of the war years gradually began to ease more and more people began to own motor cars and were far less dependent on public transport. The country's citizens were no longer content to spend their leisure time and holidays patronizing their local resorts.

Newbiggin-by-the-Sea

Cobles 'between fishing trips'. Only eight boats remain of a fleet that once numbered almost a hundred vessels, fishing out of Newbiggin. In Winter the boats catch crab, lobster and prawns. From June and over the following three months the boats catch salmon and lobster.

They now possessed the means and the desire to travel further afield –
and who could blame them? They wanted to broaden their horizons –
see a little more of 'the world'. At first they largely confined themselves
to British resorts – Filey, Morecambe, Scarborough, Yarmouth, Skegness
or Blackpool. Later it was Illfracombe, Newquay, Torbay, St Ives and
Eastbourne. Eventually and inevitably they set their sights even higher
and continental resorts beckoned seductively. Incredibly cheap holidays
abroad, beginning in the '60s, particularly to Spain and the Balearic
Islands, cast their spell and the British holidaymaker was 'hooked' –
permanently! Far bigger resorts than Newbiggin were to suffer as a
result of their former patrons' newly found spirits of adventure and it
became increasingly difficult for the 'home market' to compete with the
fantastic bargains available abroad. For example, Spain and Majorca
offered two weeks' holiday (including flight), with half-board
accommodation, in a three star hotel, with swimming pool and regular
in-house evening entertainment, for the same price as five nights' bed
and breakfast in a medium grade guest house in Whitley Bay, Seahouses
or Spittal. Moreover, the mediterranean resorts had many other
attractions to offer which Joe Public and his lady wife found difficult to
resist. But, above all, they offered three things which their UK
counterparts could not. Firstly, the attraction of the flight and in the
early days, at least, this was most definitely an attraction. Most
'ordinary' people had never been on an aeroplane in their lives and many
probably never expected to find themselves airborne: it was a very long
time before this novelty wore off, if, indeed, it ever did. Secondly, there
was the cost: the figures speak for themselves. Small resorts in the UK
found it difficult to compete with the prices on offer abroad and Joe
Public likes a bargain as much as the next man. And finally, there was
the weather. Mediterranean resorts could virtually guarantee 'wall-to-
wall' sunshine, seven days of every week throughout the holiday season
of late Spring and the entire Summer. Nowhere in Britain could
confidently promise three consecutive fine days and here, on the east
coast, a chilly east breeze off the sea could spoil even a sunny day and
peg the temperatures to between 50 and 60 degrees Fahrenheit.
There are dozens of Newbiggins around our coastline; small, hospitable,
attractive little resorts that rely almost exclusively on their beaches and
the amenities centred around their seafronts.

Half a century ago these delightful little resorts were a Mecca for families with limited resources, without their own means of transport and even more limited opportunities. But the world has moved on apace since the '40s and '50s and people's aspirations, certainly so far as holidays are concerned, are boundless. Once it was Bamburgh, Bridlington or Brighton: now it is Benalmedina, Barbados or Bali: Saltburn, Seaton Carew and Seahouses have lost out to Salou, Sousse and Sri Lanka. Torquay has given way to Torremolinos and the palm-fringed beaches of Thailand. Morecambe hasn't quite the same ring as the Maldives or Mexico. Would your children prefer Filey or Florida… go on, ask them: I dare you. I am not suggesting that the entire seaside holiday industry here in the UK is on the point of collapse. There will always be enough people who prefer to spend their holidays 'at home' to ensure this doesn't happen. But the fact remains that millions of British people do travel abroad every year and these are people who, once upon a time, would have been content to spend their 'annual fortnight' somewhere in the UK. To their credit our resorts, in latter years, have begun fighting back and all power to their individual and collective elbow. But I believe that, realistically, they will never win 'the war': their 'glory days' are behind them – but you have to admire their effort, however belated. They may well win smaller battles but they can never hope to overcome their biggest disadvantage – the weather. Years ago, someone told me that after I had gone swimming in the Mediterranean I would never again swim in the North Sea. I spent the first twenty-five years of my life swimming in that particular stretch of ocean and though the water was extremely cold you got used to it. But he was right: there simply is no comparison and I have never swum in the North Sea since. My point is that when people have experienced the warm sunshine of Majorca or the Algarve, Cyprus, Malta or Turkey or the hundred and one other venues that lure the British holidaymaker, year after year, why would they willingly return to a completely unpredictable climate. Why swap 90 degrees plus for 50 to 60 degrees? Why voluntarily exchange twelve or even fourteen days of glorious sunshine and a tan to die for for who knows what? Why give up the certainty of shorts and sleeveless shirt for the distinct possibility of long trousers and a wool jumper?

33

The truth, however unpalatable, is that Newbiggin and the hundreds of other Newbiggins have had 'their day in the sun' and will never recover their former prestige and popularity. Some of the larger resorts are, at last, coming to terms with the realisation that the holidaymaker of the year 2000 is a far different creature from his 1950s counterpart. Resort managers are doing their best to accommodate the needs and expectations of those families who, for whatever reason, still choose to spend their holidays 'at home'. Nevertheless, their abiding concern must be (as the song says) 'how you gonna keep 'em down on the farm after they've seen Paree'? It's as well that Newbiggin, even in her heyday, was never entirely dependent on tourism for her survival. There was the coal-mine and the fishing; but the mine has long since closed and the fishing appears to be in terminal decline – yet Newbiggin survives, without many tourists, without miners and with very few fishermen. Whatever else, this interesting, friendly little town is resilient.

Even with its many navigational aids a fishing boat needs help to reach the beach.

Newbiggin proudly boasts the oldest operational lifeboat station anywhere in the British Isles and Ireland. The Duke of Northumberland provided the first lifeboat and boathouse, here at Newbiggin, in 1851 and this is when the lifesaving service began here. Since that time Newbiggin has had a succession of lifeboats. The first was the "Latimer": the last off-shore boat, the "Mary Joicey" arrived in 1966 and was withdrawn in 1981 when, following a national review of lifeboat cover she was replaced by a faster in-shore craft. The first motor-powered lifeboat, the "Augustus and Laura", arrived at Newbiggin in 1938, prior to that boats ploughed their way through rough seas relying solely on the strength of the oarsman's arm. Before the arrival of the first lifeboat tractor, in 1949, the boat was launched 'manually', a term which singularly failed to recognise the vital part played by women shore-helpers in the launch and recovery of the lifeboat. On occasions stormy waters made it impossible to launch the boat in the bay and it had to be hauled, physically, overland for as much as two miles to find a reasonably sheltered cove where it might safely and more easily put to sea. Fortunately occasions as desperate as this were rare but when they did occur these spirited women unhesitatingly joined their menfolk in doing whatever was necessary. Modern technology is very much a part of today's sophisticated lifeboat and at Newbiggin this current craft carries VHF radio, satellite navigation, night visual equipment and all the other accoutrements needed for an effective service – all a far cry from the early days when rescues resulted from little more than raw courage and a seaman's navigational instincts. Over the century and a half since the service was first established in Newbiggin many, many rescues have been carried out and many lives have happily been saved. Fittingly, the bravery of many of the men responsible for these rescues, during that time, has been properly recognised by the award of appropriate medals and inscribed scrolls. The awards are justly deserved and proudly accepted but the men of the RNLI seek neither glory nor reward and nor, I suspect, are they particularly seeking either thanks or recognition.

They risk their lives voluntarily from a rare sense of duty and a compelling desire to save the lives of fellow mariners who often through no fault of their own have found themselves in perilous situations. Even those unwary sailors who, through a mixture, perhaps, of inexperience and foolhardiness expose themselves recklessly to the many often hidden dangers of the sea and whose irresponsible actions consequently endanger the lives of these brave souls are nevertheless assured their very best endeavours. The Institution, as it is generally known, receives no Government grant or financial assistance in any form: it relies entirely on the generosity of the public to support its work. There are all kinds of causes both at home and abroad worth supporting but few, I imagine, where men are prepared at all times and in all circumstances to lay their lives on the line, resolutely and unselfishly, without a thought for their own safety and entirely without ulterior motive. Ladies' Guilds, throughout the area and throughout the year, work ceaselessly by raising funds to support Newbiggin Lifeboat Station. Without their dedicated and continuous efforts and the money they raise from flag-days, fetes and open-days, the lifeboat service, both here at Newbiggin and, indeed around our entire coastline could neither continue nor survive. Commonsense suggests we must never allow that to happen.

Photographed by kind permission of the Royal National Lifeboat Institution.

The Church of St Bartholomew   (Newbiggin-by-the-Sea)

The town was originally called South Wellerick. After the Danish invasion in 875 the town was renamed Neubegang or Newbegining, with various different spellings until we finally arrive at Newbiggin. There is evidence of an ancient Saxon Chapelry here, believed to have been built by the monks of Lindisfarne and used by them in their mission throughout Northumbria and on their journeys to and from Tynemouth Priory and Whitby. The present church has 13th century origins. Once the 'daughter' church in the Parish of Woodhorn with Newbiggin, St Bartholomew's became the 'mother' church when St Mary's at Woodhorn was declared redundant in 1973. The church is smaller than it once was. It did not enjoy a happy post-medieval history. The nave is of six bays and although the north and south aisles were both destroyed after the Middle Ages their arcades remain intact. By the beginning of the 19th century both aisles were still missing and the chancel (eventually restored in 1845) was a roofless shell. Giving great dignity to the north aisle (finally rebuilt in 1913) is a splendid collection of more than a dozen medieval tombstones or grave covers, mostly 13th century, set into the wall between the windows. They are richly carved with floral crosses, a sword, shears and keys and a chalice. During the Second World War the church roof was badly damaged and its windows were blown out by mines exploding on the rocks.

The Church of St Bartholomew   (Newbiggin-by-the-Sea)

The church has 13th century origins. During the Second World War the roof was badly damaged and the windows were blown out by mines exploding on the nearby rocks. St Bartholomew's situation is quite remarkable: away from the town, on a rocky headland called Newbiggin Point it stands conspicuously in a treeless churchyard, close to the sea. The lower part of the tower is 13th century: the belfry and distinctive stumpy, stone spire was set up a century later, the spire being the only medieval example of its kind in Northumberland apart from that on the Church of St Lawrence, in Warkworth.

The Church of St Bartholomew   (Newbiggin-by-the-Sea)

The following photographs of grave covers found inside St Bartholomew's Church are all featured by kind permission of the Vicar, Reverend J M Grieve.

Some of the (13th century) medieval grave covers to be found on the
north wall of the nave and in the south porch.

The Pele Tower
(Cresswell)

W W Tomlinson described it as **"one of the finest specimens of the fortified mansion-house in the county"**. The date of the Tower is uncertain. Leonard C Leach writes; **'An early manuscript states that Sir Robert de Cresswell possessed an estate in Cresswell in 1191, which would date the Tower to the 12th century, certainly not later than the 13th century'**. Robert Hugill relates that **'the Cresswell family are mentioned in records as far back as the reign of King John, at the beginning of the 13th century, and the Tower was built by them at that time'**. Professor Nikolaus Pevsner believes the Tower to be of the late 14th or 15th centuries. It has a barrel vaulted basement-byre which was entered by a massive, iron-studded door: a circular stone staircase lead to the two upper storeys. The first floor was divided into two apartments, each with a contemporary fireplace. There are the outlines of two doorways which gave access from the adjoining manor house. In one corner of the upper chamber is a garderobe (a medieval 'privy') in the thickness of the wall. The floor of the top storey is gone. The narrowest side of the Tower faces the sea and has a turret at the north-east corner. The embattled parapet was added in the 18th century when a manor house was built adjoining the north side of the Tower, now believed to be inadequate for the needs of the family. The manor house was demolished at the beginning of the 19th century, soon after A J Cresswell-Baker built his fine Hall at the nearby Cresswell Park. All that remains of the manor house is its pedimented front doorway (on the right of the picture), now part of a field wall. The Hall, which was built between 1821-25 (and was designed by the London architect John Shaw) was itself demolished in 1937.

'This hoary and picturesque old Tower has its mysterious visitant', writes Tomlinson by way of a prelude to his reciting the well-known story of 'the White Lady of Cresswell'. The incident, central to the story, goes back to Saxon times when an earlier fortification stood on the site of the present Tower. The principal characters in the tale are the lovely daughter of a local noble and a Danish Prince whose family were long-time enemies of the Saxon lord. The two young people were sweethearts and the Prince had promised to carry her away 'over the foam'. One day the girl was standing on the turret of the tower, gazing expectantly out to sea when she saw her lover arrive on the nearby shore. However, his arrival had also been noticed by the girl's three brothers who attacked the unfortunate Prince and slew him, mercilessly, before her very eyes. Grief stricken the desolate young woman thereafter refused all food and drink and in a very short while she died from starvation. Now, according to local legend, the ghost of this broken hearted young lady can occasionally be seen, staring out to sea, on the turret of the present ruin.

The east and north sides.

At the far right end of the wall can be seen the pedimented doorway of the old manor house – all that now remains of the former living quarters of the Cresswell family before the house was demolished at the beginning of the 19th century.

42

The Hall (Cresswell)

The Hall was built from designs by the London architect, John Shaw, between 1821-25, though the actual work was supervised by the Newcastle architect John Green. Constructed from the finest sandstone, brought by shipping from quarries on both sides of the River Wansbeck, near Ashington, and from Cleaswell Hill, many of the blocks weighed as much as four and even eight tons "and were so exquisitely chiselled that the joints between them are scarcely perceptible". The walls of the house were more than three feet thick. The most detailed, comprehensive though rather technical description of this magnificent building I can find is written by Reverend John Hodgson (1832) which is reproduced in its entirety in Frank Graham's "Old Halls, Houses and Inns of Northumberland" (1977). Another detailed account is found in Leonard C Leach's publication "The History of Cresswell, Ellington, Linton, Lynemouth and Woodhorn" (1986). Both these articles are suitably illustrated with both exterior views of the Hall and interior pictures though, personally, I find the reproduced prints by T M Richardson and A Shaw in Graham's book, of greatest interest. For me, at least, they completely and successfully convey the grandeur of this magnificent establishment – both the building itself and its superb setting. While I have included one photograph of the old Hall I can see no good reason to repeat a fulsome description of the interior of the house, fascinating though this is, since others have already done so and especially since the house was demolished in 1937 and there is so little of it left to excite the imagination of anyone gaining access to what is now only a ruin. Nevertheless, as the Hall was the principal feature of this small village and as I have included both the village and a picture of the Hall in my chronicle it would be remiss, even unforgivable, of me not to give a brief description of it.

This photograph is reproduced from a very old postcard.

The entrance of this truly majestic residence was on the west side (which, as a matter of interest, was over eighty feet in length), in the centre of which was a portico topped by an entablature supported by two fluted columns. The entrance doorway lead into the hall which was separated from the staircase by a stone screen. The staircase is described by Tomlinson as **"the chief internal feature of the house"**.

The east front (which is more than ninety feet long) overlooked the sea and though without columns had a nine feet wide stone terrace which ran the entire length of this side of the house. The south front measured 107½ feet. It had a range of nine windows "and had the uniformity of its line interrupted in the centre by the bow of the music room". The entablature over the bow was supported by two pillars similar to those of the portico on the west side. Either side of the bow the centre, ground-floor window has pilasters and a pediment. The north front, as is so often the case with so many fine houses, was the least prepossessing of the four. The back staircase and several relatively unimportant rooms were situated on the north side of the Hall. Warm air, to heat the house, was carried from an underground furnace through all the passages. For any reader wishing to read more about the interior (particularly) of this fascinating structure I can thoroughly recommend the two works mentioned earlier.

The Church of St Bartholomew   (Cresswell)

St Bartholomew's was originally a 'district church' within the Parish of Woodhorn and is of neo-Norman design… ie with bell-cote, nave and lower chancel. Consecrated in 1836 the church was built specifically to serve the spiritual needs of the Baker-Cresswell family (who owned the nearby estate and Hall) and their estate workers. Two modern windows in the south wall of the sanctuary (the chancel) are dedicated to members of the family and show their gaily coloured coat-of-arms, which include sheaves of corn and squirrels. The porch is surmounted by a cross and above the architrave the figure of the Madonna and Child. On each side, below the roof, there are five corbels carved in the shape of human heads. On the chancel (east) end of the church there are no fewer than nine such carvings and a half one where the water-pipe descends. There are an additional three corbels carved with floral decoration. Strangely, the process is not repeated on the north side of the building where only five corbels are fashioned as heads, two have the floral decoration and six are blank. Leonard C Leach theorised that **"the mason must have tired of carving heads"**.

The Preceptory   (Low Chibburn)

The Low Chibburn estate was given to the Knight's Hospitallers (the
Order of St John of Jerusalem) in 1313 – 1338, we read, the community
numbered eleven souls. Revenue from the estate provided funds to help
the Order defend the states set up in the Holy Land by the Crusaders.
The Knights Hospitallers had a duty to care for the sick and shelter any
pilgrims who stayed here on their way to Lindisfarne. In the 1540s
Henry VIII closed all the monasteries in England – a period known as the
Dissolution. The work of the Knight's Hospitallers here at Chibburn was
suppressed: the land reverted to the State and was eventually given to
the Widdrington family, whose castle, built in c.1341 and demolished
c.1775, once stood about a mile south-west of here. Nothing at all
remains of the castle which was situated immediately east of the present
Church of the Holy Trinity: the site is marked by a low green mound
approached by a row of lime trees known as the Twelve Apostles. In the
1550s, Sir John Widdrington built a Dower House here at Low Chibburn
– the most complete part of its ruinous remains is the west range: the
buildings were arranged 'around a small court with the chapel on the
south'. A Dower House was often built on the estate of a widow's late
husband, where she might spend her remaining years in comfort. In
1691, Jean Bart (a French Admiral), after the battle of Dunkirk, sailed up
the east coast of England but, finding no ships in Newcastle, continued
north. On sighting Widdrington Castle from Druridge Bay a French
party was landed. They ransacked Widdrington Village and the Castle
and on their way back to their ship they torched the Dower House of the
Lady of Widdrington.

Described as 'the most complete example of a preceptory of the Knights of St John of Jerusalem in England'. Built in the 14th century, it was made into a mansion house after the Reformation, its chapel being divided into two floors and given a picturesque chimney, but the chapel lost its roof in the nineteenth century and the rest of the building has been allowed to fall into ruin. The remains of the chapel (1313) are on the right: the Dower House (c.1550) is on the left.

The remains of the Chapel from the east, looking west.

The Dower House (left) and the Chapel (right).

The west wall of the Dower House is almost intact.

Coquet Island

Despite its small size (sixteen acres in area and a quarter of a mile long) Coquet Island has been a place of sanctuary ever since the time of St Cuthbert. In 684 Elfleda, Abbess of Whitby, persuaded Cuthbert to accept the bishopric offered him by her brother, King Ecgfrith of Northumbria. The peace of the island has offered refuge to monks and hermits alike in their search for solitude. A Danish hermit, St Henry of Coquet (known as "Henry the Hermit"), who, after his death was buried at Tynemouth, established a monastic cell here in the 12th century. A decision, finally, to place a light here on Coquet Island was taken in 1839 and the lighthouse was built on top of the ruins of a medieval tower (listed in the 1415 record of castles, fortalices and towers) shortly afterwards. The unusual, square-towered, eighty feet tall lighthouse was first lit on October 1st, 1841 and its castle-like appearance is no accident: it was designed thus on the express instructions of the Duke of Northumberland (to whom the island belonged, he having purchased "Cockett Island" from John Widdrington, in 1753) to complement Warkworth Castle, a mile or so north of Amble. The lighthouse was once looked after by Grace Darling's brother and it is believed that in coming to visit him here Grace contracted the tuberculosis which was later to cause her death. In the time of the Civil War Charles I garrisoned the island with 200 men and seven guns but it was captured by the Scots, in 1643, who then "placed a garrison of their own men therein". The remains of the Benedictine cells (-a small Benedictine Monastery existed here as early as 684) are incorporated with the Keeper's house. Boats ferrying the curious and the interested alike, regularly ply their course the mile and a half from Amble Harbour but, to prevent disturbing the nesting birds, landing on the island is not permitted. More than seventeen thousand pairs of puffins nest in burrows across the island, each rearing a single chick. In excess of two hundred eider ducks also nest here, each laying six to eight eggs.

The roseate tern – one of the rarest breeding seabirds in the United Kingdom – nests on Coquet Island. Around thirty to forty pairs – more than 50% of the entire UK population – are to be found here. Fulmars, kittiwakes and black-headed gulls all contribute to the 20,000 pairs of seabirds nesting every year on Coquet Island – many travelling from as far away as Africa to return to the same nesting site they had used the previous year. There are no longer lighthouse keepers on the island. After a century and a half the lighthouse became fully automated in 1990. Though still owned by the Duke of Northumberland the island is now managed by the RSPB as a nature reserve. RSPB wardens live and work here during the Spring and Summer months conducting surveys, conserving the island's habitat, monitoring the bird population and so on. During the remainder of the year Coquet Island is inhabited only by its wildlife. Nikolaus Pevsner's observation is an interesting one: he says – **"The castellated, whitewashed buildings and the medieval remains, which have not been whitewashed, together make up an unusual and evocative group on this bleak, island site".**

The eighty-feet tall, square-towered lighthouse; once looked after by the brother of Northumbrian heroine Grace Darling, was opened on the 1st of October, 1841. Photographed by kind permission of the Royal Society for the Protection of Birds (David Barratt, Reserve Manager).

The Lighthouse

The view of the lighthouse from the south-west. It was built on the top of the ruin of a medieval tower.

Photographed by kind permission of the Royal Society for the Protection of Birds (David Barratt, Reserve Manager).

Amble-by-the-Sea

"Oh, Amble is a fine town, with ships upon the bay;
And I wish with my heart I was only there today…"

Amble developed as an exporter of coal mined at the neighbouring
collieries of Radcliffe and Broomhill. Vast quantities of coal were
shipped from Amble to Southern England and the Continent, especially
in the latter part of the 19th and the beginning of the 20th centuries. By
the 1920s, for example, more than seven hundred vessels were handling
in the region of three quarters of a million tons of coal a year. But the
coal fields have gone now; the collieries have closed and this lucrative
trade, upon which much of the town's prosperity was founded, no longer
exists. Boat building and repair work does still continue, however –
down near the harbour, the most colourful and busiest area of this
'friendliest of ports'. A harbour probably existed at Amble as far back as
the fourteenth century. The present harbour was built in 1839, at a cost
of almost £200,000. Since then it has been altered and improved when,
shortly before the beginning of the Second World War, an Act of
Parliament appointed Warkworth Harbour Commissioners to "improve
the mouth of the river". More than four hundred 'cobles' (inshore
fishing boats unique to the north-east coast), each hand-crafted, have
been built in Amble over the years. Now, the local boatyard specialises
in the repair of lifeboats from all round Britain's coastline.

The busiest and most colourful   Landing the catch.
area of this 'friendliest of ports'.

(Amble-by-the-Sea)

At the mouth of the river is a very long, stone breakwater terminated by a little lighthouse.

The Marina   (Amble-by-the-Sea)

The Marina which was opened in 1987, provides berths for no fewer than 250 craft.

It was constructed by reclaiming part of the old riverbed and the outer boundary incorporates one of the original timber jetties from the early harbour.

The Castle   (Warkworth)

The first castle at Warkworth was a Motte and Bailey type. Henry, son of David I of Scotland, was created Earl of Northumberland in 1139 and it was he who either built the first castle or, more likely, strengthened the existing Motte and Bailey castle by adding a stone curtain wall. In 1157, Henry II granted the castle to Roger FitzRichard, whose descendents held it for almost 200 years before it passed into the hands of the Percys. Roger died in 1177 and was succeeded by his son Robert, a wealthy man who did much to strengthen the castle. He built the Great Gateway which, though later altered, still stands to testify the excellent workmanship of the period. He built the Carrickfergus Tower (named after his estates in Ireland) and improved both the Great Hall and chamber – originally built by Henry, the first Earl. Robert also improved the Chapel in the bailey and the houses within the bailey walls. A stone Keep must have been built about this time "though there are no certain remains of it". The present Keep is believed to be late 14the century (or possibly early 15th century) and considerably altered in the 16th century and restored and refaced by Anthony Salvin between 1853-58. When John of Clavering died in 1332 he had lost most of his estates (including Warkworth) and had no heir to succeed him: it was then the castle became the property of the Percys. It was during the time of Henry, the fourth Earl, that the entrance to the Great Hall was heightened by a tower and its front decorated with the stone panel (still to be seen) upon which is carved the "Percy lion" – which gives its name to the Lion Tower. Much work was carried out at Warkworth during the lives of the 5th and 6th Earls. A staircase was built in one of the towers (possibly the Lion Tower): the north curtain wall was rebuilt; the Great Hall and houses in the bailey were repaired; work was done on the Keep and the Chapel window frames were repaired. The south wall between the Amble Tower and the Great Gateway was rebuilt and a new drawbridge, over the moat (built with timber from Acklington), was constructed.

The Keep.

Photographed by kind permission of English Heritage.

The Castle   **(Warkworth)**

The Lion Tower

From a window in the Keep.   From the Bailey

Photographed by kind permission of English Heritage.

Henry, the sixth Earl, died childless and gave all his estates to Henry VIII. It was twenty years before his nephew, Thomas Percy, succeeded the Earldom but Thomas was executed in York, in 1572, for his part in the Catholic "Rising in the North", in 1569. Henry the eighth Earl, succeeded his brother. At this time the Keep was still habitable though other parts of the castle were beginning to deteriorate – the Carrickfergus Tower, for example, was "in utter ruin and decay" and an inventory of the castle's furniture showed this to have been "scanty in the extreme". A letter from Lord Burghley (Elizabeth I's Lord High Treasurer) complained that Sir John Forster, the Warden of the Middle Marches, 'was plundering the castle for his own use'. Henry (the eighth Earl) died a prisoner in the Tower, in 1585, having been charged with high treason. The nine Earl (another Henry) was also committed to the Tower for his complicity in "the Guy Fawkes Plot" and, during this period, Percy leased the castle to Sir Ralph Grey of Chillingham. The Percys had long since ceased to reside at Warkworth. Grey never lived there and, through his neglect, allowed the castle to become even more ruinous: it was "used as a fold for cattle and its gates left open both by day and by night". The castle's continuing decay was almost inevitable. In 1644 it was captured by the Scots who remained there until the following year when the castle was handed back to the tenth Earl. Parliamentary troops occupied it in 1648 and did further damage. In 1672 the widow of the eleventh (and last) Earl gave John Clarke, the estate auditor, permission to remove what was left of the once-proud fortification. Taking that noble lady at her word he proceeded to cart away no fewer than 272 wagon loads of stone, timber and lead with which to build himself a manor-house at Chirton, near North Shields About the middle of the 19th century Algernon, the fourth Duke, repaired the Keep and part of it was made habitable. He also repaired other parts of the castle in an effort to prevent further decay. In 1922, the eighth Duke placed the castle in the care of the Department of the Environment: it is now one of the English Heritage's 409 'historic sites'.

The Castle   **(Warkworth)**

Unusual views of the Bell Tower.

Photographed by kind permission of English Heritage.

(Left): The Bell Tower (Right): The Lion Tower

Photographed by kind permission of English Heritage.

The Gatehouse.

Photographed by kind permission of English Heritage.

The Castle   **(Warkworth)**

(Right to left): The Amble or Montague Tower: The Lion Tower: The Bell Tower: The Gatehouse: (- extreme right): the Carrickfergus Tower

Photographed by kind permission of English Heritage.

The Bridge-Tower and Bridge End House   (Warkworth)

The fourteenth century tower, one of the very few bridge-towers to be built anywhere in England and the mid-18th century, five-bay house of two-and-a-half storeys situated at the north end of Bridge Street.

Bridge End House   **(Warkworth)**

Situated in Bridge Street, on the northern edge of the village, the house is, without doubt, one of the finest to be found in Warkworth. Indeed, Pevsner goes further and describes it as **'the best house'** in the village. It is a mid-18th century dwelling, two-and-a-half-storeys with five bays and quoins. The lower two floors have an original eaves cornice below the second floor, which was added in the latter part of the 18th century. There is a good, pedimented doorway on the south front and, separating the whole from the street, an excellent, contemporary wrought-iron gate and railings.

The Bridge-Tower

Very few bridges in England were ever fortified and this is the only bridge-tower to be found in Northumberland. It is a small, simple gateway at the south end of the bridge: its purpose was to defend the narrow passageway. Unfortunately, its parapet and machicolations have long since disappeared.

The fourteen century bridge has two ribbed, segmental arches (of sixty feet span) and sharp, triangular cut-waters. John Warbuton, writing in 1715 described it as **"a goodley bridge supported by two arches in the middle whereof an ancient cross with ye arms of ye Percies thereon"**. The cross referred to was, sadly, thrown into the river in 1830 and has never been recovered. Another writer, more recently, relates – **"Before entering Warkworth the (river) Coquet must be crossed by a quaint, many angled bridge of two arches, rebuilt in 1379. It was formerly embellished with a pillar bearing the Percy arms"**.

The Church of St Lawrence   (Warkworth)

The first record of there being a church here in Warkworth is in 738
when Ceolwulf, King of Northumbria, gave "Wercewode" and the
Church of St Lawrence to the monastery of Holy Island. The present
structure dates from the 12th century and stands on the site of the old
Saxon church, some remains of which were discovered during restoration
work in 1860 – the angles of the earlier building and a length of walling
four feet thick. A Saxon cross is preserved in the recess of the south wall
of the chancel. In 1174 a Scottish army of William the Lion and lead by
Earl Duncan invaded and ravaged the village. The terrified inhabitants –
men, women and children – took refuge in the church, which the barbaric
invaders then proceeded to burn to the ground. The occupants all
perished: at least one hundred persons met their deaths in this shameful
deed; some reports have put the number dead as high as 300. A very
large number of human bones, thought to be those of the victims, were
found inside the church during the alterations (already referred to) of
1860. The new church, built after this ungodly defilement, is a mixture
of architectural styles. The north wall of the nave and chancel are
Norman, as are the windows in the nave. The tower belongs to the
Transitional period. The stone spire (-the only other medieval example
like it in Northumberland is to be found on St Bartholomew's Church,
Newbiggin-by-the-Sea) is of the Decorated period. The vestry is
probably Early English. The south aisle and porch were added during
the Perpendicular era. The room above the porch, incidentally, was used
as the village school until a century or so ago.

Embleton Towers   (Embleton)

The most substantial part of the present house dates from 1828 and was
designed by Newcastle architect John Dobson… for the vicar, the
Reverend G D Grimes. Dobson refaced the south-western end of the
adjoining Tower, inserting new windows: he also built a large extension
with handsome reception rooms overlooking the garden. Best known as
a classicist in this instance the architect chose to work in a restrained
neo-Tudor style so advanced for its time that the former vicarage is often
taken for a Victorian rather than a Georgian Building. For his new
additions Dobson used the local whinstone – hard to work but extremely
durable. He provided extra insulation of lath and plaster under the main
floors and skilfully planned his entrance lobby to intervene between the
main entrance hall and the draughts and winds from the front door. The
conservatory (right) has a roof consisting of arched, cast-iron ribs.

Photographed by kind permission of Mr K Seymour-Walker.

The Tower   (Embleton)

It was built in 1395, allegedly at a cost of £40 (forty pounds). The Tower forms the east wing of the present building "and may have begun as a more conventional house… in the early 14th century before being remodelled later in the century". The 'Turris de Emildon', as it was described in the 1415 list of castles, fortalices and towers, was a necessary place of refuge. Only recently a marauding band of Scottish raiders had "lain in the fields of Emildon and did great destruction". Various additions and alterations were carried out to the building over the ensuing centuries until by the late 18th century (if not earlier) the Tower again became a wing of a larger house (ie the Vicarage). Perhaps the greatest change of all was made in 1828 when "a large and handsome wing" was added from designs by the celebrated Newcastle architect, John Dobson: this increased considerably the size of the Vicarage. The Tower is remarkable for having two vaulted chambers in the basement, divided by a central wall. Although the Tower is now entered from the modern wing it seems likely the original entrance was on the first floor. The newel staircase connecting the upper rooms has largely disappeared though some of the old fireplaces remain and some of the windows, though blocked, are still traceable. Projecting spouts, for roof drainage, still exist.

The Tower   **(Embleton)**

By the 18th century the Tower once more became a wing of a larger house. The oddly elongated Tower which forms the east wing of the Old Vicarage may originally have been a 14th century house before it was remodelled as a Tower later in the century.

The Tower is attached to a 'modern' house though it is likely the entrance may have been on the first floor as there is a blocked opening on the north wall.

Photographed by kind permission of Mr K Seymour-Walker.

The Church of the Holy Trinity   (Embleton)

Basically a 13th century building though extensive repairs and alterations were carried out to the church firstly between 1803-05; these included a new roof and ceiling for the nave, re-flooring with flags, repairing the pews and building the churchyard wall. It may also have been around that time that the 13th century chancel was replaced with a simple Georgian structure with a low, flat, white-washed ceiling. Another addition at this time was the Grey gallery at the west end of the north aisle. "Despite all of this work there was continued unease." In 1849 a meeting was convened "to consider the condition of the church and the necessity of re-seating it, repairing the roof and floor thereof". In 1849-50, the Newcastle architect, John Dobson, who some twenty years previously had carried out extensive alterations to the vicarage next door, was employed to carry out further major restoration of the church – extensions of the nave aisles as far as the west wall of the tower; the extension of the north aisle (which became the Grey porch); the replacement of all the windows by ones with 19th century 'middle pointed' tracery; the replacement of the nave roof, but, apart from some strengthening of the south aisle, the aisle roofs were left as they were. Dobson demolished the Vincent Edwards and Grey galleries; the Craster porch was taken down and rebuilt on the same foundations but higher than before. In the lower portion of the tower the architect inserted a ceiling supported by stone arches the springers of which were designed to rest in the spaces of some early Norman windows which, unfortunately, Dobson saw fit to block up.

The Church of the Holy Trinity (Embleton)

The Church dates from the early thirteenth century although, over the years, many alterations have been made to the building culminating in the re-roofing of the nave and a new chancel being built in the middle of the nineteenth century.

In a paddock, a hundred yards
north of the Church of the
Holy Trinity, stands an 18th century
dovecote, built of red brick
with a pantiled, pyramid roof.

In the back garden of number 4,
Sunny Brae (one of a row of
cottages in the south end of the
village, looking east towards the
sea) stands a centuries old
dovecote: circular, of sandstone
rubble and 'with a convex
profile'. Pevsner believes it to be
no later than of the 17th century
and **'it might'**, he says,
'even be medieval'.
Graham claims that in 1425 it
had a stone wall built around it
(- long gone) **"at a cost of
sixteen shillings"**.

The Hall

The little medieval 'Turris de Howyke', mentioned in the 1415 list of fortalices, castles and towers to be found in Northumberland and owned at that time by one Emeric Hering, was demolished when the present 'dignified, classical house', which replaced it, was built in 1782 for Sir Henry Grey, from designs by the Newcastle architect, William Newton. Part of Howick has belonged to the Grey family since 1319 but the first of the family to live here (in the ancient Pele) was Sir Edward Grey – who came from Morpeth in 1597. In 1518 it was described as **"a little pile, a mile from the shore"**. The south front of the present building (- much of the house was remodelled after a disastrous fire in 1926) is nine bays wide with a slightly projecting three-bay, pedimented centre. The ground floor is rusticated. The two upper floors of the centre piece have four giant, unfluted, Ionic attached columns. Prior to the alterations of 1809 the driveway lead up to the main entrance which then was on the south front. In that year, however, George Wyatt moved the entrance to the north side of the house and a Tuscan, one-storey addition was made there to receive the new entrance hall. Wyatt also terraced the south front of the house: the upper terrace is balustraded, the middle terrace a simple stone wall. Howick Hall is said to be "one of the finest and largest houses in Northumberland" though, sadly, the main central part of the block is no longer occupied: Newton's west wing is used as the present house. The grounds and gardens – which are open to the public for much of the year – are especially attractive… **"The lawn sweeps in a magnificent slope to the margin of a fine trout water which (flows) through the shrubberies and plantations… The gardens are… enriched with every species of native flowers… on which Flora has bestowed a more than ordinary richness of scent or beauty of appearance". "The park is well-wooded, with beeches, elms and firs and the trees and shrubs, of all kinds, round the Hall are magnificent."**

The magnificent nine-bay south front with its four giant, Ionic
columns and huge pediment enclosing the Grey coat-of –arms.
The upper terrace with its balustrade and the middle terrace with
the simple stone wall can be seen at the front of the house.

Photographed by kind permission of Lord Grey.

The five-bay east front and the driveway from the main road that once led to the main entrance at the (south) front of the house.

The west front, with its ground floor rustication, window pediments and architraves.

The Hall (Howick)

The north front:

Originally, the driveway led to an entrance on the south front. This was changed c.1810 by George Wyatt, when the north side became the main entrance. When the entrance was transferred a one-storey Tuscan addition was made for the entrance hall.

William Newton's west wing is used as the present house.
Photographed by kind permission of Lord Grey.

The Village (Craster)

Pevsner described the village as **"picturesque but disappointing architecturally"**. To be brutally honest the only three features likely to attract the interest and attention of the visitor are the small harbour, overlooked by a row of white-walled cottages (which, to be fair, on a sunny day is a very pretty sight); the 'kippery', which still produces the succulent, world-famous Craster kippers but which, for several reasons, not least the dictate of the Health and Safety Executive and the natural disinclination of Mr Robson, the owner, to allow every curious Tom, Dick and Harriet invading his premises and getting in the way of both his busy workforce and the process of 'smoking' the kippers, is not accessible to visitors; and, thirdly, the lovely Craster Tower, a 'lived-in' house well outside the village and half a mile from the sea. In any case, like the kippery, it too is not open to members of the public so can hardly be counted as one of Craster's attractions.

I have, smugly perhaps and tantalisingly certainly, included the latter simply to show my readers what they are missing!

The Harbour (Craster)

As far back as the early years of the 17th century men have sailed from Craster to fish the sea – though very little fishing (mostly crabs and lobsters) is done from here now. The present harbour was built between 1906-10 by the Craster family in memory of a brother killed on active service in Tibet, of all places. The harbour entrance with Dunstanburgh Castle in the background.

The Craster family has lived here since at least the twelfth century. Edmund Craster was the owner in 1415 but Albert, the founder of the Craster 'dynasty' was in possession of Craster before 1168. As members of the same family are still living in Craster Towers today (June, 2002) this means that Albert's descendents have occupied the Tower for almost nine hundred years. The three-storey, five-bay 'new house' was added to the south side of the Tower in 1769.

Photographed by kind permission of Mrs J Michael and Miss Mary D Craster.

The three-storeyed, battlemented Tower (the battlements, incidentally, are a fairly modern addition) certainly existed as far back as the beginning of the 15th century – it is mentioned in the County's list of castles, fortalices and towers compiled in 1415. It has a ten feet high, vaulted basement and a wheel-stair in the south-east corner where a wall is almost six and a half feet thick. The adjacent east wing has four feet thick walls which, Pevsner believes, suggest a medieval or 16the century date but this part of the Tower was extended and remodelled in the nineteenth century.

Photographed by kind permission of Mrs J Michael and Miss Mary D Craster.

The south front, with quoins at both ends, is faced with square whinstone and it has a central, open pediment. The windows have heavy architraves and the central window above the doorway, is pedimented. Many of the house's characteristics suggest the hand of Newcastle architect, William Newton – the floating cornice above the central, second-floor window, for example, is also a feature of Shawdon Hall (near Glanton), which many believe is also the work of Newton. The central doorway is tripartite, with Tuscan pilasters, and it, too, is surmounted by an open pediment.

Photographed by kind permission of Mrs J Michael and Miss Mary D Craster.

The Smoke House (Craster)

A typical, mid-19th century smoke house with its whinstone walls, pantiled roofs and wooden ridge ventilator.

Photographed by kind permission of L Robson & Sons.

Cleaning and preparing the fish.

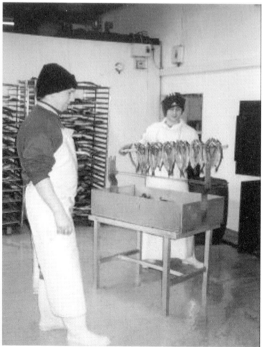

Ready mounted and waiting to be hung – the fish, that is!

Waiting their turn to be cured.

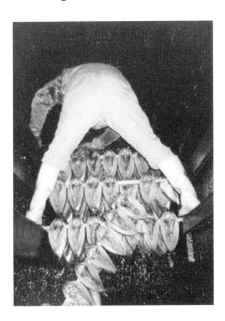

A smouldering mixture of white wood shavings topped with oak sawdust cures the kippers and gives them the unique taste that only Craster kippers enjoy.

The Castle   **(Dunstanburgh)**

Photographed by kind permission of English Heritage.

The Castle   (Dunstanburgh)

The castle stands on the Northumbrian coast some seven miles north-east
of Alnwick. It was built during the reign of Edward II by his cousin, the
Earl of Lancaster, but it was barely completed when armed opposition to
Edward resulted in the Earl's being executed as a traitor in the Hall of his
castle at Pontefract. A later owner, John of Gaunt, made considerable
alterations to strengthen the castle, then his son made himself King, as
Henry IV and Dunstanburgh became a royal castle governed by
Constables. The castle at Dunstanburgh is the largest in Northumberland
and includes an area of more than ten acres (ie the land encompassed by
the Curtain Wall). The ending of "burgh" suggests that at one time it
was an Anglian fortified settlement. In early Norman times
Dunstanburgh formed part of the Barony of Embleton, which belonged
to Odard of Bamburgh, Sheriff of Northumberland in 1121. After
Odard's death it was confirmed by his son, John, by Henry I, in 1133,
'for the service of three knights'. In 1255 the barony, including
Dunstanburgh, was exchanged with the famous Simon de Montford, Earl
of Leicester, for lands elsewhere. No doubt Earl Simon appreciated the
strategic value of the solitary hill whereon now stands the castle's ruins.
It may well have been his intention, one day, to build himself a fortified
refuge on this rather remote spot – but he never did. After Simon's death
at the battle of Evesham, in 1265, his fortified lands were confiscated by
Henry III to be later granted to his second son, Edmund ('Crouchback'),
Earl of Lancaster, in 1269. Edmund died in 1296 to be succeeded by his
son, Thomas, also Earl of Lancaster – High Steward of England and
cousin to the now reigning Edward II. There was no great love lost
between the two cousins and on close examination it must be said that
both men were rather unsavoury characters.

Part of the south curtain wall, from the Constable's Tower east towards the Egyncleugh Tower.

Edward cared nothing for the duties of a king. His only desire was to use the many advantages of his position to enrich his friends and amuse himself. It is said he kept very low company, especially at Court, and deliberately avoided his natural counsellors – the Barons. His arrogant behaviour and dissolute lifestyle led eventually to him being deposed and in 1327 he was cruelly murdered in the dungeon of Berkley Castle. By 1311, Earl Thomas had five earldoms in his possession and an immense private army at his command. By all accounts he was a greedy, vicious and grasping man implacably opposed to Edward and his court favourites. It was he who, in 1313, ordered preparations to be made for the building of his castle at Dunstanburgh. Perhaps, like Simon de Montford, he viewed the site as a place of refuge in time of future need. Lancaster's defiance of Edward, always smouldering on the surface, came to a head when, in 1314, he and three other Earls refused to accept the King's summons to give service against the Scots. Edward's campaign was a total disaster. The English army, three times the number of the enemy, were totally defeated at the Battle of Bannockburn. Far from being a glorious adventure, designed to placate his restless and critical barons his defeat at the hands of Robert the Bruce assured Scotland of her independence and strengthened the position and influence of the Earl of Lancaster. Meanwhile, the Earl's great castle at Dunstanburgh was under construction. By Michaelmas, 1314, a great part of a large moat, eighty feet wide and eighteen feet deep, had been dug on the west side of the castle. The gateway, too, was progressing – Spanish iron had been purchased for the hinges and the 'cramps' for binding the stones together. Carts and wagons constantly brought loads of timber, lead, stone, sand and mortar and sea-coal for burning the lime, was brought from Newcastle. This was a scene of constant activity – and perhaps not a little urgency! So much so that a hostelry, eighty feet long and twenty feet wide, was erected to house the great number of skilled craftsmen and labourers needed – masons, carpenters, smiths, plumbers, lime-burners and carters; all under the instruction of one Master Elias, the master builder.

In August, 1316, King Edward, rather surprisingly considered the relations that existed between the two cousins, granted Thomas a licence to strengthen his castle at Dunstanburgh with a stone curtain wall and to crenellate it and 'to hold it without interference'. As the greater part of the construction was completed already it would seem Edward's licence either simply made legal the work already done or else it marked the completion of the walls and gatehouse. The years immediately after the crushing defeat at Bannockburn were testing years indeed. Edward's position was critical. Lancaster was all-powerful. The Scots ravaged the north of England; private warfares broke out in several parts of the Kingdom and England was caught up in the worst famine in European history: chaos ruled. By 1318, however, there was some small measure of reconciliation between King Edward and his Earl of Lancaster – but Edward was king in name only, his every act was controlled by a Standing Council. Weak and largely disregarded though Edward was he had by this time recovered from the humiliating shambles of Bannockburn and he was not prepared to accept further humiliation designed to be of a particularly long term nature. Edward was determined to reassert his royal position and avenge himself on his enemies. In 1321 he suffered a further setback when he was compelled to exile his two closest supporters. In 1322, however, 'the tide turned' and he was, at last, able to destroy the main centres of opposition to royal power. Lancaster, through his own stupidity in failing to support those of his allies opposed to the King found himself isolated. He further compounded his stupidity by inviting Robert the Bruce to come to his assistance with a Scottish army. This treacherous act alienated him even further and the long suffering north countrymen defeated what was left of his great private army at the Battle of Boroughbridge. Before his defeat and capture the Earl had been urged to escape to Dunstanburgh, while there was still time. He declined to take this sound advice and lived only a very short while to regret it. King Edward took swift and terrible revenge for the years his cousin had heaped insult and humiliation upon his royal person.

Lancaster's head was hacked off in the Great Hall of his castle at Pontefract and, immediately following the execution, his castle at Dunstanburgh was committed to Roger Horsley, the King's Steward in the north, with instructions to deliver it to Richard of Embleton, a wealthy Newcastle merchant. Thereafter, the castle was placed in the care of other Constables – notably John Lilburn (who gave his name to the picturesque Lilburn Tower, built while he was the castle Constable) and Roger Mauduit. Repairs were carried out in 1351 and in 1380 the castle became the property of John of Gaunt, son of Edward III. He too made important alterations and repairs. He blocked the entrance to the gatehouse with a stone wall, effectively turning it into a Keep. He made a new gatehouse, complete with Tower, portcullis and barbican, on the west side and built a strong battlement wall around the Keep. John of Gaunt died in 1399 when both the castle and the Barony of Embleton passed to his son who, in September of that year, became King Henry IV. The Wars of the Roses, which were to spell eventual doom for the castle and its usefulness, were fast approaching. Much destruction was wrought upon the castle in several sieges during this period. Some small repairs were carried out in 1470 but after that year expenditure upon it almost ceased. The Royal Commissioner of Henry VIII, in 1538, reported the castle to be "very ruinous, of small strength, and with no buildings standing except the Keep – and that needed a new roof". In 1550 it was said to be "in wonderful great decay", but no repairs of any consequence were made. Other castles, nearer the border, were considered most important and worthy of much greater attention and Dunstanburgh was eventually abandoned.

Lilburn Tower.

Probably built for John Lilburn, constable of Dunstanburgh, about 1325, on the highest point of the castle enclosure. It measures about 30 feet square, externally, has walls six feet thick and is three storeys high.

The Castle   **(Dunstanburgh)**

In 1314 Thomas, Early of Lancaster, began to dig out the moat and the construction of the Gatehouse was also begun. Thomas was later executed in 1322. Around to the left of the Gatehouse, on the west side, John of Gaunt built a new gatehouse, in the 1380s, "to provide a more conventional but still heavily defended entrance to the castle". Lancaster's Gatehouse, with its two drum-towers separated by an arched entrance passage, then became the Castle Keep.

Photographed by kind permission of English Heritage.

The Egyncleugh Tower lies in the south-east corner of the curtain wall and dominates a narrow inlet from the sea, called (in the old days) 'Egyn Cleugh'.

The Castle

The south curtain wall runs in a straight line, west, from the Egncleugh Tower some hundred and eighty feet to the Constable's Tower but is interrupted midway by an oblong turret which projects seven feet into the moat.

Photographed by kind permission of English Heritage.

The mid-18th century church (c.1740) which was enlarged in 1792. The
tower and spire, which is described as 'a conspicuous landmark' and
'rises like a lighthouse from a ring of crocketed pinnacles' are both of the
later date. The octagonal screen at the base of the spire, with its
quatrefoils* and grotesque heads, looks 18th century but was actually
added in 1860. (* four leafed or pointed ornamental figures)

The present church, of 1746, replaced one on a nearby site and is a simple but attractive village church.

St Ebba's was rebuilt in 1860.

The Tower   (Beadnell)

The three-storeyed Pele Tower stands in the centre of the village.   It dates back certainly to before 1587 for in September of that year Thomas Forster of Adderstone Hall made a will leaving it to his eldest son, Matthew, the "profytt" of it to go to Matthew's mother, "untyll it please God to send him of lawful age" (- presumably until he reached his majority). The Tower was to remain in the hands of the Forster family for the next three hundred years. By 1818 it was reduced to little more than the back premises of an old inn, formally the Black Bull – it is now the Craster Arms. It retains much of its original masonry and is in excellent condition though the interior has been largely modernised. The basement, now used as a beer-cellar, is vaulted. The remains of the newel staircase, which lead to the next floor, still exist but the stairway is blocked except for a part at the bottom used for storage. The outside of the Pele Tower was restored in the 18th century. The two-bayed south frontage is adorned with the coat-of-arms of the Craster family and large, stone, foliage traits (which critics have suggested are somewhat out of proportion). The motto reads, "Dum Vivo Spero" – "Where there is life there is hope". Until recently the lead sign of a Newcastle insurance company, with the insignia of three castles and the number 7058 was also attached to the front of the building. In the old days fire services were controlled exclusively by these companies who would only attend fires in buildings bearing their plaques. Alas, when I photographed the Tower in March 2002, the plaque had been removed.

The old Pele Tower – now the Craster Arms.

A raven surmounts the family coat-of-arms. The raven, or crow, is a pun upon the family name, which formerly was spelt 'Crawster'. To choose a 'punning device' was a common practice in earlier times.

The Hall   (Beadnell)

Beadnell Hall is a late 17th century, possibly early 18th century house. The south front has three storeys with five bays. On three sides of the building later 18th century Gothic had been added, with castellated gables and typical quatrefoils and broad-pointed sash windows. The windows have architrave surrounds. The stone porchway has a heavily moulded pedimented door surround. The east end of the hall was once a medieval tower, the home of the Harding family (who became landowners in Beadnell as far back as 1383). The offices to the west, including the coach-house and servants' quarters (now a public house) probably date from the 18th century. In 1701, the building – the property of one William Forster, the largest landowner in Beadnell – was known as East Hall. In 1735 the Hall came into the possession of Thomas Wood (possibly the grandfather of John Wood, who, in 1798 commissioned the construction of Beadnell's lime-kilns). Internally the house has been altered at various times but still boasts good late 17th century or early 18th century panelling in four rooms.

The office to the west, including the coach-house and the servants'
quarters, probably date from the eighteenth century.

This rather strange and incongruous 'wing' was added to the Hall at the beginning of the twelfth century. Castellated, with three bays on the west front and five on the south it is an extension of the main building and its rooms (dining-room, kitchen and so on) are connected directly to the apartments at that (east) end of the Hall.

The twentieth century 'wing' which, on first impression, seems a strange and entirely unsuitable addition has a certain attraction and is not without interest. Two-storeyed, of five bays: those to the extreme left and right of the first floor are 'blind'. The ground floor windows are broad-pointed, arched, sash-windows alternating in size. All the windows have architrave surrounds.

The Lime Kilns   (Beadnell)

In 1798 Richard Pringle built the first kiln here at Beadnell for John Wood, of Beadnell Hall, whose nearby estate was to supply both the limestone and the coal needed to burn it: one load of coal was used to burn two loads of limestone. The kiln, which was 24 feet high, had a pot measuring sixteen feet in diameter at the top and nine feet in diameter at the bottom. The kiln was confidently expected to produce one thousand cartloads of lime each year which would be exported to other ports around the British Isles from the adjacent 18th century harbour, which Wood duly extended to cope with this increased trade.

The Kilns from the shore.

Such was the success of John Wood's venture that a second and third kiln was built on the site and a tramway was constructed to bring the coal and limestone to the top of the kilns.

Photographed by kind permission of the National Trust

The tiny harbour at Beadnell is the only harbour on the east coast which has its entrance facing due west.

The Harbour   (Seahouses)

North Sunderland Seahouses, as it used to be called, appears to have had
little to commend it over the years nor has it been overly blessed with
enthusiastic admirers. W W Tomlinson described it as **"a malodorous
place, where fish-curing is extensively carried on"**. An extension of
North Sunderland it was developed from a haven for fishing and lime-
burning activities. The original harbour works are in large blocks of red
and grey sandstone (of a period c.1786): later modifications were made
and new piers were built at the end of the 19th century. A bank of lime-
kilns, built close to the harbour for the convenience of loading and
unloading, line the south quayside. These, together with the fish-trade
prompted Walter White to describe Seahouses, in 1858, as **"a small,
common-looking town; squalid in places"**. Pevsner (1992) observes
that **"the centre of the village is sadly altered to cope with the tourist
trade"**. The harbour area on a sunny day is a picturesque sight and is
now where thousands of tourists, every year, climb aboard the vessels
heading for the Farne Islands and the sightings of seals and the many
sea-birds. But, remembering, from personal experience, what a
charming, unspoilt little village Seahouses was, even thirty years ago, it
is difficult not to sympathise with Pevsner's restrained comment: there
are many others who would express their opinion with considerably more
vigour.

A picturesque sight on a sunny day.

"Cuddy's ducks"; St Cuthbert's ducks" or, to give them their proper ornithological title, Eider ducks (though it is the male bird which is the more colourful of the two: the female bird is a rather plain, brown colour) fishing contentedly in the harbour waters.

The lime trade ceased early in the second half of the nineteenth century: the kilns are now used as fishermen's store houses.

The Island's most conspicuous feature is the "white painted and extremely pretty" lighthouse, built in 1809.

The tower and lantern of the lighthouse.
Photographed by kind permission of the National Trust.

The tiny chapel of St Cuthbert – who died on the island in 687 – was built c.1370 and restored in the middle of the 19th century. Its early 16th century slates, oak panelling, stalls and screens all came from Durham Cathedral.

Photographed by kind permission of the National Trust.

Inner Farne   **(The Farne Islands)**

Some of the remarkable 16th century oak panelling etc, brought to St Cuthbert's Church from Durham Cathedral by Archdeacon Thorp, in the middle of the 19th century.

Photographed by kind permission of the National Trust.

The Memorial to Grace Darling, who lived on both Brownsman and Longstone islands and who died in 1842, inside the Church of St Cuthbert on Inner Farne.

Photographed by kind permission of the National Trust.

Photographed by kind permission of the National Trust.

Before the building of the present lighthouse a fire was lit at the top of the stone pele tower built by Prior Castell of Durham, c.1500.

The east side of the Prior Castell's Tower overlooking the Church of St Cuthbert. At one time there was another church, St Mary's, across the small courtyard to the south. In the bottom left corner of the photograph is a 15th century font which quite possibly originated in this ancient chapel of which practically nothing now remains.

Hundreds of pairs of Puffins (or 'Sea Parrots', as they are sometimes called) nest every year on Inner Farne. Indeed, the birds on the Farne Islands and those on Coquet Island, further down the Northumbrian coast, form the largest concentration of Puffins anywhere in the United Kingdom. The Puffin nests in a burrow and lays only one egg. When the chick is six weeks old is it abandoned by its mother and left to fend for itself. The Guillemot lays its single egg on a bare rock. However, because of the 'pear shape' of the egg it is extremely difficult to dislodge it from its 'nest' even in a strong wind.

Photographed by kind permission of the National Trust.

A pair of nesting Arctic Terns.

These little 'Sea-Swallows', as they are sometimes called because their tails are very like those of our agile summer visitor, are fiercely protective of their nests and will dive repeatedly at passing intruders who stray too close, their needle sharp beaks inflicting pain and often drawing blood from unprotected arms and heads foolishly left uncovered.

A nesting Eider Duck. The Eider lays between six and eight eggs and is locally known as Cuthbert's or "Cuddie's" duck after St Cuthbert.

Staple Island   **(The Farne Islands)**

You can almost smell Staple Island before you see it. Here nest
hundreds and hundreds of puffins (sometimes called the 'Sea Parrot' or,
to give them their local name, 'Tommy Noddies'), Guillemots and
Kittiwakes. A low, squat tower once used as a beacon – until it was
destroyed by fire in 1783 – still exists on the island.

Photographed by kind permission of the National Trust.

The lighthouse on nearby Brownsman was abandoned when its replacement was built on Longstone. The work began in 1825, with stone quarried in Yorkshire and brought north, by sea, in sloops (small, one-masted boats). The tower was completed in December of that year and then the lantern was erected. The new light first shone on February 15th, 1826, at which time the light at Brownsman was finally extinguished.

Photographed by kind permission of the National Trust.

Ida's great ancient fortress towers over the sleepy village of Bamburgh below its walls.

The Castle   (Bamburgh)

Bamburgh is a natural and almost impregnable fortress probably
occupied by the Romans during their occupation of this part of
Britain. The Britons gave it the name 'Dinguardi'. In 547 it was
seized by Ida the Flamebearer, an Angle chieftain who eventually
established himself at Bamburgh and formed a settlement that was
to become the nucleus of the powerful Kingdom of Northumbria.
His grandson, Ethelfrith, gave the fortified settlement to his wife,
Bebba, and it became 'Bebba's burgh' – thus Bamburgh. In 744 it
was described thus: **"Bebba is a most strongly fortified city, not
very large, being the size of two of three fields, having one
entrance hollowed out of the rock, and raised in steps after a
marvellous fashion"**. T H Rowland tells that **'the complete
enclosure extends to some eight acres'**. In Angle times
Bamburgh was a communal fortress: in Norman times it became a
private stronghold. Before the invasion of 1066 the population
was one race and mainly free. The Normans were conquerors who
reduced the English to a position of serfdom. Their great castles,
therefore, were private fortifications, primarily intended to defend
the owners or occupiers against their own serfs – the local
population. As the position of power of the Ancient Kingdom of
Northumbria declined in the ninth and tenth centuries the 'castle' at
Bamburgh slowly decayed. In the tenth century it was twice stormed by
the Danes. "The pleasure her dignity afforded us is past and gone," wrote
a monk in the eleventh century. In 1095 Robert de Mowbray, the third,
Norman, Early of Northumberland rebelled against the King, William II
(William Rufus). William led an army north and overran
Northumberland. Mowbray was a virtual prisoner in his stronghold at
Bamburgh. Realising he couldn't storm the fortress William ordered his
men to 'make another castle' before Bamburgh which he called
'Malvoisin' – meaning 'evil neighbour', though the 'castle' was, in fact,
a siege-works. William Rufus fortified his 'castle' strongly with his own
men then retired south. Mowbray, taking advantage of the King's
absence, sneaked out of Bamburgh and headed for Tynemouth, which
castle, unknown to him, the King had already taken – and the Earl's
brother also.

Viewed from the south-west.

View from the south-east.
The castle has been rebuilt and added to many times since the Middle Ages. Between 1894 and 1904 it was restored and repaired by Lord Armstrong whose efforts were sneeringly dismissed by one critic who spoke of the restoration as **'the acme of expenditure with a nadir of intelligent achievement'**.

Photographed kind permission of Mr F. W. A. Watson-Armstrong

The garrison from William's 'malvoisin' pursued the fleeing Earl and captured both him and his companions. On learning of Mowbray's arrest King William ordered the Earl to be taken to Bamburgh and unless the castle be given up (it was being held by the Earl's wife in the absence of her husband) Mowbray should have his eyes put out: the castle duly surrendered. In 1164 the stone Keep was built at a cost of four pounds and in 1168 a further thirty pounds was spent on the castle works. The Keep stands fifty-five feet high and is sixty-nine feet, north to south and sixty-one and a half feet east to west. Its walls are massive – eleven feet thick on the front and nine feet thick on the other sides. The stone with which it was built was quarried at North Sunderland and the stones are unusually small, probably to make their transport easier (by men and pack animals). The eight acres enclosed by the outer curtain wall are divided into three baileys – the Keep stands in the middle bailey. In the seventeenth century Bamburgh Castle came into the hands of the Forster family who squandered their estates with reckless extravagance. They were declared bankrupt and all their lands were put up for sale. In 1704 these were purchased by one Nathaniel Crewe, Bishop of Durham. Lord Crewe married Dorothy Forster but died childless and his wealth was distributed to various deserving charities. One of the trustees of these charities was Archdeacon Sharp. He altered and restored the castle in the late eighteenth century and established a girls' school there. After a period of another hundred years there was increasing alarm over the dilapidated state of the building. **"Considering its important historical association"**, reads the statement in Northumberland County History, **"it cannot honestly be said that the present state of the castle is satisfactory"**. Lord Crewe had bequeathed ample funds ' intended to raise again her fallen dignity' and make her the "pride and glory of the people of Northumberland". An indication of the castle's wretched state lies in the fact that it possessed 'paste-board battlements'. Shortly after these complaints were made the castle was purchased by the first Lord Armstrong (the munitions magnate who built Cragside house, near Rothbury) who restored and rebuilt it at considerable personal expense.

The Keep (right of centre) is the oldest part of the surviving castle. It was built in 1164 at a cost of thirty pounds. It stands fifty-five feet high, measures sixty-nine feet north to south and sixty-one and a half feet east to west. Its walls are eleven feet thick on the front and nine feet thick on the sides.

The stone to build it was quarried at North Sunderland.

Photographed by courtesy of Mr F W A Watson-Armstrong.

Grace Darling's grave (Bamburgh)

On the 7th of September Grace and her father, William, set off in raging
seas from Longstone Lighthouse to rescue the survivors of the steamer,
'Forfarshire', which had been battered on the notorious Harcar Rock –
one of the smaller Farne Islands – a mile or so away. Having herself
survived this terrible ordeal she died four years later, on October 20th,
1842, from tuberculosis, at the tragically young age of 26. She lies in
this low-railed plot with her father William, her mother Thomasin
(d.October 16[th,] 1848), her brother Job (d.December 6th, 1830 at the age
of only twenty) and her sister Thomasin (d.August 13th, 1886 at the age
of seventy-eight). William died in 1865 aged seventy-nine years.

Grace Darling's Houses

Opposite the Church of St Aidan is the humble little cottage (now Horsley Cottage) where Grace was born in 1815.

The house where Grace died is a grey stone building by the green – now the post office (on the left).

The monument enshrines a stone figure of Grace, her hair falling over her shoulders, a carved oar by her side – it is a copy of the original effigy by Raymond Smith (1846) which, owing to the adverse effects of the elements, is now preserved inside the Church of St Aidan.

It is quite likely that the present structure stands on the site of the church where St Aidan died, on August 31st, 651. Nothing now remains of this ancient Saxon church. The square west tower is 13th century but, architecturally, the church's outstanding feature is the unusually long chancel with its fine blind arcade of pointed arches, built c.1230. The nave has two arcades of four pointed arches and dates from c.1200. On the north wall of the chancel is both a piscine, under a pointed arch, and a low side window – a narrow opening through which people who suffered from infectious diseases could receive communion. Among several monuments to be found inside the church the original monument to Grace Darling is to be found here. It is a stone figure, her hair falling over her shoulders with a carved oar by her side. The canopied monument in the churchyard is a copy. Another interesting feature of the church is the 13th century vaulted crypt, beneath the chancel. It consists of two chambers separated by a wall into which a little Saxon sundial has been inserted. The crypt was discovered, quite by accident, in 1837, when some decayed oak planks were being removed from the chancel floor. Five coffins of the Forster family were found on a stone shelf at the east end of the crypt; one contained the remains of Ferdinando Forster who was murdered by a neighbour from Rock, on the streets of Newcastle, in 1701; another was that of General Thomas Forster, whose dramatic escape from Newgate Prison, in 1715, was due in no small part to the efforts of his devoted sister, Dorothy.

Church of St Aidan   (Bamburgh)

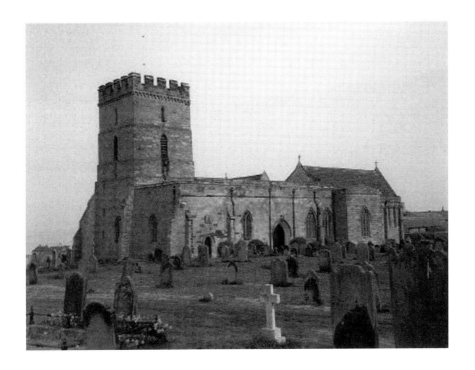

St Aidan's is said to be one of the three finest Parish churches in Northumberland – the others are in Alnwick and Norham. Its origins date from 635 when St Aidan arrived on Lindisfarne from Iona. The present building is 13th century and the chancel, measuring sixty feet, is believed to be the second longest in the country. It contains magnificent reredos in Caen stone. The original effigy of Grace Darling is situated in the north aisle. Her memorial in the churchyard is sited so that it can be seen by passing ships.

The Grace Darling Museum   (Bamburgh)

A bronze inscription on the wall reads "This building was erected in
memory of Grace Horsley Darling (1815-1852) one hundred years after
her heroic rescue, with her father, of the survivors of the steamer
'Forfarshire', wrecked on the Farne Islands, on 7th September 1838".
The museum preserves many relics associated with Grace but pride of
place goes to the coble used in the rescue. This open rowing boat,
twenty-one feet long and six feet wide was built at Tweedmouth c.1830.
It was still in use at the Longstone Lighthouse (from where the Darlings
set off on their rescue mission) until c.1873 when it was sold to John
Joicey who placed it on his ornamental lake at Newton Hall, Stocksfield,
near Hexham. In 1913 it was donated to the Royal Lifeboat Institution.
Other of Grace's possessions on display include a lock of her hair, the
cup she used, fragments of a dress, a pair of her slippers, her beaver
bonnet, presented by the milliners of Berwick, a velvet armchair given
her by the Duchess of Northumberland, medals, paintings and
mementoes from the stricken vessel.

Photographed by kind permission of The Royal National Lifeboat Institution

On a promontory called Guile Point, at the northern extremity of Ross Sands, on the north Northumberland coast, south of and immediately opposite the harbour of the island of Lindisfarne, there stands two tall, slender, tapering pyramids of red sandstone ashlar.

These two obelisks stand in an east/west line and are some five hundred feet apart.

Photographed by kind permission of the Brethren of Trinity House, Newcastle.

These beacons, brick built and on a sandstone base, were built by John Dobson for Trinity House, in 1820. The east beacon (67 feet high) cost £135 to construct: its west neighbour is some 83 feet high and cost £186. Inside the outer sandstone shell are the original timber beacons still in surprisingly good condition. Around 1930, however, the west beacon was struck by lightning and its upper timbers are now charred. The beacons, which are 'listed', were last renovated in 1992. On one face of the westernmost beacon is a stone tablet on which is inscribed "Repaired 1916: Capt. E W Kent, Master: Capt. J C Hardy, Deputy". There is another tablet, on a different face of the same beacon, which reads "Restored 1937: Capt Brown, Master: Capt Hardy, Deputy".

"At the south-east corner of Holy Island, crowning a curious, conical rock, which rises a hundred feet above the sea, is the picturesque Lindisfarne Castle." The castle was originally built c.1550, from stone taken from the nearby monastery after the Dissolution. During the Civil War it was first of all held for the King and then for Parliament. In the 1715 Uprising it was held, very briefly, by the Jacobites. It was after the Civil War, however that the castle began slowly to decay although a garrison of Royal Artillery was stationed here as late as 1820. After that it was converted into a Coastguard Station and later it became the headquarters of an Island Detachment of the Northumberland Artillery Volunteers. By the end of the 19th century it was in very poor condition indeed. Edward Hudson, the owner of 'Country Life' magazine bought the castle in 1902: the outside walls were still complete but the inside was derelict. Sir Edward Lutyens set about restoring the castle 'as a home to live in'. Fortunately the architect displayed the good sense not to make wilful alterations so that its outward appearance, at least, has not changed a good deal over four and a half centuries. In 1944 the owners, Sir Edward and his sister, Miss G de Stein, gave the castle and its contents to the National Trust. The entry hall is completely modern and leads to two, plain, vaulted chambers – the dining room and the Ship Room. On the second floor are bedrooms facing south and east. The rooms are filled with a fine collection of, mostly oak, early 17th century English and Flemish furniture.

Lutyens subtly improved the external appearance of the castle by
removing its crenellations and rounding the edges, thus simplifying the
silhouette and emphasising the impression of a stone sea-bird crouching
on its nest of rock, just like fulmars which nest on the ledges of the crag.

Fishermen's Store Sheds **(Holy Island)**

A set of store-sheds at the base of the castle are, literally, "boat-houses".
Originally, they were a Norwegian fishing boat used on the celebrated
'Shetland Bus' escape route across the North Sea from occupied Norway
during the Second World War. The vessel was brought down to
Lindisfarne and sawn into three sections and then installed, upside down,
as a row of sheds.

These, with their little weather-boarded doors, writes Pevsner, even now
'look quaintly habitable'.

The Lime Kilns   (Holy Island)

The lime kilns on Lindisfarne were built in the 1860s by a company from Dundee seeking to extract the island's limestone. The coal used for the burning of the stone was brought down from Scotland. Poor quality coal was satisfactory for lime burning: around 1800 this was costing seven pence per load while 'smithy' coal cost twelve pence (one shilling) and house-coal was eleven pence per load. The kiln structure consisted of six lime-burning pots. To the rear of the kilns was the embankment of the railway which carried the limestone to the kilns from quarries on the north side of the island. The railway also brought the coal from and the burnt lime to a jetty situated at the west of the castle – fragments of the timber jetty can still be seen. The enterprise had ceased operation by 1896 – only the kilns remain. T H Rowland gives a detailed account of 'Limestone Burning' in his book "Discovering Northumberland: a Handbook of Local History" (F Graham, 1973): I am obliged to him for much of the following information. The commonest form of kiln was a square of semi-circular tower built into a hillside or a ramp. They were usually some fifteen to twenty feet across and of similar height. Within the kiln structure was an oval or circular bowl some ten feet in diameter and lined with brick. The sides were parallel, internally, for six to eight feet downwards from the top then they tapered towards the bottom where there were grates each with two flues. Lime was important for a number of reasons. It was spread on fields as a kind of manure. It was used for building purposes and for lime-washing the exterior walls of farmhouses (using brushes made from marram grass), though this was a custom more widely practised in the counties of Yorkshire, Durham and Cumberland and rarely seen in Northumberland. It was also considered to be a valuable cleansing agent and cow-sheds, for example, were given a thorough lime-wash at least once every year. Kilns burned turf and even fern, as well as wood and coal. While chalk took approximately twenty-four hours to burn limestone took some sixty hours. **"The kilns of Holy Island,"** concludes Rowland, **"must have produced very large quantities of lime and their smoking mouths must have been a feature of the coastline. They were well known as a place of warmth and light"**.

Photographs of the Castle and Lime Kilns by kind permission of the National Trust.

St Aidan's Statue   (Holy Island)

Aidan arrived from the tiny Scottish island of Iona in 634 to help Oswald
spread the Christian faith throughout his kingdom of Northumbria.
Oswald was immediately impressed by the obvious sincerity of this
gentle, self-effacing man – who was unable to speak a word of the local
language and had to rely, in the early days at least, on the King himself
to act as his interpreter. Oswald offered the Bishop any part of his
kingdom where he might establish his community of monks: Aidan
chose the lovely island of Lindisfarne, some five miles off the
Northumbrian coast. Three factors are generally recognised to have
influenced the monk's choice: firstly, the island reminded him so much
of Iona; secondly it enabled him to maintain easy communication with
the King in his Royal City of Bamburgh, without him living in the
constant, suffocating shadow of his friend and benefactor; but it was
mostly, one supposes, because Lindisfarne offered not only a measure of
security (being cut off from the mainland twice every day by the tide) but
solitude and the opportunity for uninterrupted meditation which, quite
clearly, was vitally important to Northumbria's new Bishop. A very
simple, very basic monastery was quickly constructed on the island, built
along the same lines as Celtic monasteries elsewhere, consisting of a few
'beehive huts' as cells for the monks, a larger 'hut' for the church and
another where the monks might share their communal meal or entertain
pilgrims or other visitors. Whether this was founded on the site of the
present ruined Priory simply isn't known. This is certainly a possibility
though it may have been built on the raised ground to the south of the
existing monastery, known as the 'heugh' – there is evidence that some
kind of building stood here at one time. Aidan impressed everyone who
met him with his humility, his simplicity, his kindliness and the sincerity
of his faith. He and his fellow monks lived an extraordinarily frugal
existence. They had no money and no possessions. Whatever gifts they
received they gave away to the poor. Aidan once annoyed King Oswin
by giving a valuable horse, given to him by the King, to a starving
beggar. Anyone who came to visit them was obliged to share their simple
fare. Aidan travelled nearly everywhere on foot. Only when his journey
was long and time important would he make an exception to his rule.

He did this so that at every possible opportunity he could converse with the people he met. If they were heathens he preached them the gospel of Jesus Christ and often baptised them into the bargain. If they were already believers he sought to strengthen their faith. From time to time he felt a compelling need to be alone to communicate with God and concentrate his thoughts in prayer and meditation. On these occasions he would sail out to the Farne Islands, some distance off shore and an hour or so from Holy Island. Here, he could be completely alone with only the sea-birds and the seals for company. Aidan was Bishop of Lindisfarne for almost seventeen years. He died at Bamburgh, next to the church which he himself had founded. It is said he died of a broken heart when he learned of the death of Oswin, King of Deira – Northumbria's southern province. When Aidan was taken ill his attendants constructed some kind of temporary 'shed' or 'lean-to', against the west wall of the church, where the monk might convalesce. Sadly, it wasn't to be. Aidan, according to Bede, was leaning against a wooden beam when he died – on the 31st of August, 651. Remarkably, his church was twice later destroyed by fire and when it was rebuilt for the third time the blackened timber was preserved in the present church as a lasting memorial to this "Apostle of the North". The monks of Lindisfarne carried his body back to their island retreat where Aidan was (initially) buried in the monk's cemetery. However, when Finan, Aidan's successor, built a more permanent church on the island Aidan's remains were transferred, as a mark of great respect, to the right side of the altar. Yet his body did not long rest in peace. When Colman, the third Bishop, returned to Iona he took some of Aidan's relics with him. King Edmund, on his return from the North, took some of the saint's bones back to Glastonbury. Finally, the rest of Aidan's remains (after several adventures and difficulties) were interred in Durham Cathedral after the monks finally quit their island home, in 875, from fear of the invading Danes. Aidan had been disturbed for the last time. In the churchyard of the Church of St Mary the Virgin stands a tall, gaunt figure of St Aidan. Eleven feet high, aesthetic of face and figure, bearing aloft in his left hand a torch that symbolises the light of the Gospel:

in his right hand his bishop's crozier. His head is framed against a Celtic cross. The statue is the work of local sculptress, Kathleen Parbury. Firstly she built the figure of St Aidan in clay. Then she made moulds from the clay and cast them in concrete. Finally, she used red sandstone as an aggregate to tone in with the colouring of the Priory Church. The statue was unveiled in the presence of Her Majesty Queen Elizabeth in 1958.

"He cultivated peace and love, purity and humility; he was above anger and greed and despised pride and conceit; he set himself up to keep and teach the laws of God and was diligent in study and prayer. He used his priestly authority to check the proud and the powerful; he tenderly comforted the sick; he relieved and protected the poor."

(Bede: 'Ecclesiastical History of the English People'.)

The old village of Holy Island is beside the harbour. In the square
(formerly the Market Place), on the green, is a beautiful stone Celtic
cross. It stands twelve feet high and was rebuilt by John Dobson at H C
Selby's expense, in 1828 – as its inscription reads. It stands on the
pedestal of 'St Cuthbert's Cross', erected by Bishop Aethelwold.

The Castle   (Haggerston)

The family of Haggerston "boasts a long, uninterrupted pedigree" and is
one of Northumberland's oldest having owned lands at Haggerston since
the 12th century. In 1311, "within the walls of their manor-house",
Edward II received homage from Thomas, Earl of Lancaster, for the
earldom of Lincoln. In 1345 Robert de Haggerston received permission
from Edward III to crenellate his mansion. The 'Turris de Haggerstan' is
mentioned in the lists of both 1415 and 1541 – when it was described as
"a strong tower in a good state of repair". Much of the building was
destroyed by fire in 1618. It was repaired, however, and by all accounts
was perfectly habitable in 1759. Nevertheless, shortly after this and
before his death in 1777 Sir Thomas Haggerston constructed a new
house "of very plain design" – two storeys high with seven bays and a
central pediment – which incorporated the old, large square tower,
formerly the family 'seat'. The Haggerstons were staunch Roman
Catholics yet, despite the religious, social and political upheavals of the
17th and 18th centuries, particularly around the time of the Jacobite
Uprisings in 1715 and 1745 they, like other notable Catholic
Northumbrian families, not only held on to their wealth and property but
were able (often through judicious marriages) to actually increase the
size of their estates. Sir Thomas Haggerston, on his demise, was
succeeded by his son Carnaby who, in 1808, extended the existing
premises by adding three-storey, three-bay wings to either end of the
main front. This extra building work – which also included domestic
offices and servants' quarters – took three years to complete. When Sir
Carnaby died, childless, the house and the estates passed to his nephew
who, in turn, bequeathed Haggerston to a great-nephew – an inveterate
gambler by the name of John Massey Stanley. Stanley accumulated such
huge debts that, eventually, he had little option but to sell his inheritance,
in 1858, to John Naylor of Welshpool for the not inconsiderable sum of
£340,000.

The Water Tower was added during the reconstruction by Norman Shaw in 1893-97.

Photographed by kind permission of British Holidays (David Eccles, General Manager).

In 1889 Naylor was succeeded by his son Christopher John Leyland – and he it was who transformed what was hitherto a fairly ordinary if substantial Georgian House into the one hundred and fifty four roomed Victorian mansion it was to become. Between 1893-97 Leyland employed the celebrated architect, Norman Shaw, to practically rebuild Haggerston (- to "aggrandize the house", as one writer colourfully described it), in much the way he had done at Chesters, near Hexham, in 1891. Shaw cleverly retained parts of the old house but altered the main reception rooms behind the original façade. He added three new wings around an internal courtyard – this more than doubled the size of the house. Within the courtyard he also designed a magnificent Great Hall. Shaw also added the 153 feet tall water-tower which, alas, is almost all that remains of the palatial mansion which was swept into oblivion in 1933. In 1908 a new stable-block was constructed which, in addition to extensive stabling, provided garage space for ten motor vehicles, servants' quarters and a staff ballroom. In 1911 the central core of the house was again destroyed by fire, whereupon Leyland, without hesitation, employed the services of Edinburgh architect, James Dunn, to rebuild the house on an even grander scale than before. The south and west fronts were completely redesigned, a porte-cochere was added and the rotunda extensively repaired. All of this cost a great deal of money and the resources to carry out these grand schemes were by no means limitless. When C J Leyland died, in 1923, he had lived in his spectacular mansion for less than twenty years. The responsibility for maintaining this vast edifice (which, by now, had become something of a 'millstone' around the family's neck) fell upon C J's son, Christopher Digby but, crippling death duties, taxes and seemingly never-ending costs proved too great a burden and Digby was forced to sell off parts of the estate and resign himself to living in only a small part of the rambling house. Attempts to raise further capital had only limited success and, finally, in 1931, the remaining 1,750 acres of the estate, and the house, were put up for sale. The buyer had no intention of living at Haggerston. Indeed, almost immediately he took steps to demolish the house and auctioned off its entire contents… staircases, fireplaces, wall-panelling, flooring – everything went 'under the hammer' and all of which can now be found in other grand houses scattered around Northumberland!

The Castle

The 153 feet tall Tower provided storage space for three huge, water tanks fed from the lake and a nearby spring – **"combining architectural drama and domestic practicality in a typically inventive Victorian manner"**.   (Faulkner and Lowery).

Photographed by kind permission of British Holidays (David Eccles, General Manager).

The Castle

In 1908 (the date is inscribed in the 'triangle' above the tall, arched doorway) a new stable-block was constructed, which in addition to the stables, provided garages for ten motor vehicles, servants' quarters and a staff ballroom. The doorways with the 'Gibbs surround' are stables; the wider doorways – of which there are five on the east and west sides of the block – were garages for motor vehicles. The canopy in the centre was simply to provide shelter for both cars and carriages when not being used. The symmetrical north face of the stable block with the tall, arched, rusticated archway at its centre surmounted by the date stone – 1908.

Photographed by kind permission of British Holidays (David Eccles, General Manager).

The Town Hall   (Berwick upon Tweed)

Designed by S & J Worrall (1754-61) though the architect, Joseph Dods, unusually, has left his name above the main entrance. The front of the hall was completed in 1754 and then extended to the rear in 1761. Tall and severe with a giant portico of Tuscan columns up a high flight of steps and behind this a 150 feet high belfry. The belfry has four stages – a square bell stage with louvred, round-headed window and four pilasters on each side: a clock stage with the clocks framed in open-pedimented surrounds: an octagonal upper stage with attached Ionic columns and an open balustraded parapet (where prisoners from the cells were allowed to exercise): and, finally, a stone spire. Described as 'perhaps the most conspicuous building in Berwick' the Town Hall is set 'on an island site' at the bottom of Marygate. The spire contains eight bells, one of which is rung as a curfew each weekday evening at eight o'clock. Four of the bells belong to the Church of the Holy Trinity, which has no tower, and which are rung for Sunday services. The ground floor of the hall is arcaded at the sides and to the rear. The top floor was once the town gaol and is still preserved as such

There is a rather nice Venetian window to the rear of the building.

The Three Bridges   (Berwick upon Tweed)

The Old (Berwick) Bridge, built between 1611 and 1625: the modern, Royal Tweed Bridge, of 1925-28 and Robert Stephenson's Royal Border Bridge of 1847-50.

Work on the old red-sandstone bridge, by James Burrell – King's Surveyor at Berwick – began c.1611 but wasn't completed (at a cost of £15,000) until c.1625. In 1799, John Fuller wrote: **"It is built of fine hewn stone and has fifteen spacious and elegant arches (- with Doric columns on many of the cutwaters). It measures 1,137 feet in length, including the land stalls. Its width is seventeen feet. At each of the pillars, which are fourteen in number, there is an outlet to both sides"**. The fact that after nearly four centuries the bridge (forty-five feet high at its highest point) is still in such remarkable condition is a tribute to the quality of the workmanship at the time it was built. The timber foundations of an older structured, destroyed by a great flood, in 1199, and afterwards rebuilt by King William the Lion, are said to be visible at low tide about eighty yards higher up the river.

The Royal Border Bridge   (Berwick upon Tweed)

Described as 'one of the finest railway viaducts anywhere in the world' the bridge was designed by Robert Stephenson (1847-50) to carry the main railway line from the south to Edinburgh: it was opened by Queen Victoria and Prince Albert on August the 29th, 1850. Built largely from stone removed from the old castle the bridge is one hundred and twenty six feet high and two thousand, one hundred and sixty feet long. It has twenty-eight arches each with a span of more than sixty feet. The piers are of rock-faced stone: the arches are brick (stone-faced). In total 1,710,000 bricks were used. Two thousand workmen were employed to build the bridge which cost more than £250,000 – a huge sum, at the time.

The Royal Tweed Bridge

Built between 1925-28 the newest of Berwick's three bridges at one time carried the main road (the A1 Trunk Road) before the construction of the town's by-pass. The Royal Tweed Bridge, though by far the least prepossessing of the town's bridges, nevertheless has four magnificent spans stretching four hundred and seventy yards (1,410 feet) – the span of the north end is 371 feet – and is, or was, the longest highway bridge in Britain. One critic has complained (not without truth) that the bridge "lacks elegance, a fact which is conspicuous because it stands beside two magnificent earlier structures".

"- a splendid street of well restored and maintained Georgian houses built immediately behind the riverside town wall."

Number 18 (with flagpole) is the late 18th century Custom House: two-storeyed with five bays; arched windows on the ground floor with a Venetian doorway. Number 21 (second from right) is a three-storeyed house with all Venetian windows on the first and second floors. The doorcase has Doric columns topped by a broken pediment. Thomas Sword Good (1789 – 1872), the painter, lived here from 1846 until the year he died. Number 22 (end right) has an interesting doorcase. The town wall separates the houses from the river.

The Church of the Holy Trinity   (Berwick upon Tweed)

The oldest church in Berwick and built on the site of the medieval
Church of St Mary. It was restored and enlarged in 1855. Quadrangular
in shape and built 'in the Italian style'. Being without either a tower or
bell-turret and having the walls of the nave carried above the roofs of the
rest of the building 'it has a somewhat singular appearance'. John Knox
is reputed to have preached here in 1548 – though not in the present
building. The Parish Church of the Holy Trinity, on Wallace Green, like
the Barracks and the Royal Border Bridge, was built with stone from the
old castle. Except for the little early Victorian chancel it was built, on
the initiative of Colonel George Fenwicke, Governor of Berwick,
between 1648 and 1653, to replace the dilapidated and undistinguished
medieval church which stood on the site of the present building.

The Barracks   (Berwick upon Tweed)

For many years soldiers were billeted around Berwick in lodgings and
inns but those upon whom the responsibility fell for this rather
impromptu hospitality began to be increasingly irritated by the
arrangement and, as a result of local pressure, the Ravensdowne Barracks
were built – they were (apparently) the very first barracks to be built
anywhere in England. Their construction began in 1717 and they were
finally occupied in 1721. The identity of the designer was long thought
to have been Vanburgh but now it has been satisfactorily established that
it was, in fact, Nicholas Hawkmoor though Andrew Jelfre, the architect
appointed by the Board of Ordnance, may well have modified
Hawkmoor's designs. The barracks are believed to have been built
largely from stone taken from the ruins of the old castle. The barracks
comprise three independent buildings, on three sides of a quadrangle :
the fourth side (- photograph) is closed by a high wall with a gatehouse.
They were designed to accommodate thirty-six officers and six hundred
men and though they have had an interesting and useful past they no
longer function as a military barracks in the way that they did for almost
two and a half centuries. They now house the spectacular "By beat of
Drum" military exhibition, which traces the history of the British
Infantryman from 1660 to the end of the nineteenth century; also the
Berwick Museum and Art Gallery and, not least, the Regimental
Museum of the King's Own Scottish Borderers. Having been military
barracks since 1721 they were the Headquarters of that illustrious
regiment from 1881 until 1964. When Ravensdowne Barracks was
completed the Board of Ordnance ran out of money and had nothing left
to furnish and equip them with such basic essentials as beds, cooking
utensils, and so on. Local innkeepers and taverners were so glad to be at
last relieved of their rather less than welcome 'guests', however, that
they willingly and cheerfully set about raising money to buy the
necessary equipment – that, in effect, would remove the soldiery from
their hitherto long occupied premises and restore them to their owners.

The Barracks   (Berwick upon Tweed)

"These buildings are very strong. They are two storeys in height, of free stone and stand on high ground east north east of the town. The situation is healthy and well aired. They compose a square 217 by 121 feet inside, exclusive of which they have two back yards with reservoirs in each for ashes and other conveniences. There are twenty-four rooms for officers and seventy-two for privates; the latter contain 576 men. There is an ordnance store, which forms the south face of the square. The north face of it (featured) consists of a guardhouse, a black-hole and a gateway, over which, on the outside, the King's coat-of-arms are exquisitely carved in stone; and in the middle of the square there is a fountain that supplies the barracks with water. There, also, and in the adjoining parade, young troops are drilled; but the punishment of flagellation is only inflicted within the square."

(John Fuller: 1799)

Across the courtyard is the tall, crow-gabled, main building (the 'Clock Block') with a recessed arch capped by an open pediment. The 'Clock Block' was built in 1739 and replaced an earlier gunpowder magazine: it now houses the Regimental Museum.

The south and east faces of the Clock Block, built in 1739 and which replaced an earlier gunpowder magazine. A particularly interesting architectural feature are the stepped gables which Pevsner described as **"archaic"**.

Part of the east block.

The two side blocks were built first: three storeys high and twenty one bays long, the buildings end in stepped gables.

The west block.

Photographed by kind permission of English Heritage

The Barracks

The fourth side of the quadrangle is the Gatehouse. The tall, plain, massive archway at the entrance to the barracks is capped by the coat-of-arms of King George I and has fine old iron gates.

Photographed by kind permission of English Heritage

Bibliography

A Guide to the Anglican Churches in Newcastle and Northumberland;
(1982)

The Buildings of England: Northumberland; Pevsner et al
(Penguin, 1992)

The History of Cresswell, Ellington, Linton, Lynemouth and
Woodhorn: Leonard C Leach (1986)

Northumberland: England's Farthest North; (Coronation edition, 1953)

Castles of Northumberland; Brian Long (Harold Hill, 1967)

Castles and Peles of the English Border; Robert Hugill
(Frank Graham, 1970)

Comprehensive Guide to Northumberland; W W Tomlinson
(Eleventh edition, Wm H Robinson)

The Old Halls, Houses and Inns of Northumberland;
(written and published by Frank Graham, 1977)

Discovering Northumberland: a Handbook of Local History;
T H Rowland (Frank Graham, 1973)

The Bridges of Northumberland and Durham;
(written and published by Frank Graham, 1975)

Durham Villages; Barry Thompson (Robert Hale, 1976)

Linden Hall, a concise History; Christopher Baglee

A Biographical Dictionary of British Architects, 1600-1840;
Howard Colvin (John Murray, 1978)

Town Trail for Morpethian:
(written by A H Tweddle from 1984 onwards)

Northern Cemetery under threat; J S Curl (Country Life; July 2nd, 1981)

Warkworth, Alnmouth, Amble, Coquet Island, Boulmer, Longhoughton
  – a short history and guide;
  – (written and published by Frank Graham, 1975)

Coquet Island; Paul G Morrison and Tony Rylance
(Belfry Publicity, 1989)

Northumbrian Castles, series 1, the Coast;
(written and published by Frank Graham, 1972)

Curiosities of Northumberland; J Armstrong, F Graham and
T H Rowland (Frank Graham, 1970)

A History of Embleton Parish Church; Oswin Craster
(Photography by George Skipper; designed by Sue Dale – no date)

Dorothy and the Forsters of Bamburgh;
(written and published by John Bird, 1982)
Tyneside Portraits; Lyall Wilkes (Frank Graham, 1971)
Medieval Castles of Northumberland; T H Rowland
(Frank Graham, 1969)
Pubs and Clubs: Licensed Premises in Blyth Valley Area;
compiled by Robert Balmer, 1999
The History of the Saints of Lindisfarne; Kathleen Parbury
(Frank Graham, 1970)
Handbook to Morpeth and Neighbourhood; D F Wilson
(first published 1966; facsimile edition Newgate Press, Morpeth; 1996)
The County Books: Northumberland; Herbert L Honeyman
(Robert Hale, 1949)
Lindisfarne, the cradle island; Magnus Magnusson (Oriel Press, 1984)
Lost Houses of Newcastle and Northumberland;
Thomas Faulkner and Phoebe Lowery (Jill Raines, 1966)
There's no town like Berwick; Rev Donald A Macnaughton
(published by the author, 1986)
The History of Berwick-upon-Tweed; John Fuller
(first published 1799; facsimile edition by Frank Graham, 1986)
Dunstanburgh Castle & Warkworth Castle;
Her Majesty's Stationery Office.

© Harry Dobson 2002

All rights reserved. No part of this publication may be reproduced
or transmitted in any form or by any means, electronic or mechanical,
including photocopying, recording or by any information storage
and retrieval system, without prior permission in writing from
Harry Dobson, Westaways, 1 High Stobhill, Morpeth, Northumberland NE61 2TT.

ISBN 0-9531840-1-3

Published by H. G. Dobson

Printed and bound by Martins the Printers Ltd,
Sea View Works, Spittal, Berwick upon Tweed